TACKLE-MAKING FOR ANGLERS

TACKLE-MAKING FOR ANGLERS

BY
L. VERNON BATES

LONDON: HERBERT JENKINS

New Edition 1953
Second Impression 1958

Printed in Great Britain by D. R. Hillman & Sons, Ltd., Frome

CONTENTS

5

PAGE

PREFACE

THE object of this book is to guide the angler in the manufacture of all those tackles which can be made at home with simple tools. It is not generally realized that an enormous proportion of angling equipment falls into this category, and there is very little indeed which cannot be made by the willing amateur.

Anyone who takes up tackle-making as a hobby will find that by so doing they enjoy a threefold advantage. Firstly there is the saving of money, a consideration which is in itself sufficient justification for a close study of the following pages.

Secondly there is the advantage of being able to indulge one's every whim as regards the design of the various tackles, and of using one's powers of invention in evolving new patterns.

Lastly it will be found that this side-issue of angling is almost as absorbing as the sport itself. Long winter evenings and tedious close-seasons can be pleasantly and profitably passed in preparing tackle for future fishing occasions.

It is indeed strange that, despite the enormous numbers of angling books, no one has yet payed any attention to tackle-making, except for short articles in the angling periodicals. Fly dressing, it is true, has several books to its credit; but artificial flies represent a very small proportion of the paraphenalia of the fisherman. A glance through the contents of the present volume will show the reader that the majority of the material is new. I do not propose, therefore, to include in my preface an apology for adding yet another volume to the long list of angler's books.

The subject matter is essentially practical and concise; consequently it is not a book which one would read for reading's sake, for unlike most anglers' books it cannot be spiced with descriptions of select waters or battles with giant fish. But the lively, enthralling interest which is lacking from the book is to be found, multiplied many times, in the hobby which it places within the reader's grasp ; a hobby which offers a deeper, more lasting pleasure than could be obtained from the mere reading of any book.

The directions for making the various tackles are so arranged that each movement or process is given in its correct consecutive order, and the reader will find that his task is simplified by following these implicitly. In the case of the more complicated patterns difficulty may be experienced in retaining a mental picture of the complete procedure, in which case the directions will appear rather involved. If this occurs, an infallible plan is to obtain the necessary materials and make each movement as directed. Immediately the whole operation will become absolutely clear.

THE ROD

THE average man, on looking in the tackle-shop window and seeing the beautifully-finished rods therein, will perhaps think that rod-building is indeed a specialist's craft and one which, even in an amateur sense, he is not fitted to pursue.

Actually, rod-building is a job which is well within the scope of any angler, even if he is not gifted with a particularly useful pair of hands. The professional product, beneath all its whipping and glittering varnish, is just a simple, straightforward piece of work which presents no difficulties whatever once the rudiments of the craft are thoroughly grasped.

Rod Timber

Rod-timber can to-day be bought in various lengths, thicknesses and tapers. Thus, straight, suitably-balanced wood can be obtained by making a careful selection from the available stock. This is a godsend to the beginner who might possibly find difficulty in successfully reducing square or parallel wood.

The woods in general use include split-cane (single and double built), greenheart, hickory, lancewood, whole cane and Spanish reed.

Of these the first mentioned is undoubtedly the best and most generally useful—but it is also the most expensive. Single-built split-cane consists of six triangular pieces of selected bamboo which are cemented together to form, in section, a hexagon. Double-built split-cane comprises twelve pieces of bamboo and is also hexagonal in shape but much stronger than the single-built variety. Both can be obtained fitted with a thin steel wire running through the centre. The wood is then known as steel-centred.

The chief advantages of split-cane are : it is strong and very difficult to break under ordinary fishing stresses ; its action, if properly made, leaves nothing to be desired ; it is not prone to warping but keeps its straightness indefinitely if properly used ; it is lighter, with due regard to its strength and pliability, than any other rod timber.

Its disadvantages are that it is the most expensive (yet perhaps the cheapest) to buy ; and secondly, if by any mischance it is broken, it is not easy to effect a repair. This is due to the fact that when breaks occur they are usually *straight across* the wood and not of the tapering variety which lend themselves to splicing. However, breaks in good cane are rare, which is fortunate as they frequently entail an outlay for a new joint.

This wood is extensively used in all types of fly and spinning rods, and of late has become very popular amongst sea-anglers.   It is also used as a tip or top-joint for bottom-fishing river rods.

Its nearest rival for the angler's favour is greenheart, a wood which occupied first place until the introduction of cane.   It is still a favourite among many anglers who find that it has certain properties which suit their individual requirements.

It is cheaper than its successor and is very nice to handle, not only in rod-building, but also in fishing.   In the smaller sizes of rods, say up to ten ounces, it is not materially heavier than cane, but in heavy salmon and sea rods the difference is very noticeable.

Thickness for thickness greenheart is slightly the weaker. It has less lifting power, is more brittle, and is subject more to warping, though not to any great extent.   Should a break occur, however, the wood can usually be effectively spliced, thus eliminating the cost of a replacement joint.

When choosing greenheart the respective pieces should be carefully tested for straightness.   The grain lines should run parallel to the length of the wood.   Any pieces with flaws or irregularities should be strictly " tabooed."

Hickory and lance-wood are rapidly disappearing, though the latter is still used in some cheap rods.   It is a somewhat unreliable wood given to warping and to sudden and inexplicable breaking, apparently through brittleness.

Hickory occasionally gives a very nice action but is also subject to distortion. To the amateur rod-builder these two can occasionally be useful on account of their cheapness, but it is unwise to use them in the thinner pieces such as top joints, etc. As butt-pieces on rods which are not required for heavy service they are quite satisfactory.

For the river bottom-fisher a lighter wood is necessary in order to eliminate the fatigue of holding a long rod for several hours. To overcome this the lower joints are often made of whole-cane or Spanish reed. Both these woods are bulky but light, particularly the latter. Their chief drawback is that they have very little taper, which makes it necessary to perform a series of splices in order to obtain the correct graduation from the butt to the top joint, which latter usually consists of a tip of greenheart or split-cane, as neither whole-cane nor Spanish reed are suitable for the purpose.

Both woods are fairly stiff and unyielding which, coupled with the more pliable tip, makes for very rapid striking. For this reason they are especially favoured by roach fishermen and river anglers in general.

Some discrimination is necessary in their selection, for good straight pieces are the exception rather than the rule. With regard to Spanish reed care must be taken to ensure that the chosen lengths are of a suitable graduation for splicing in their consecutive order. To reduce splicing to a minimum choose, where possible, those pieces with the greatest taper, providing that they are straight.

Spanish Reed is a very fragile wood which will not withstand any severe strain, but in every other way it is particularly suitable for rods for bottom-fishing.

Selected whole-cane is stronger and heavier though not quite so bulky and is therefore occasionally adapted for use for the butt-joints of light sea rods and pike rods. This purpose it serves admirably and at a great saving of money, though the rod so fitted is sometimes a little top-heavy.

When purchasing rod-timber the angler should pay as much as his pocket will allow in order to obtain the best quality. There is a great disparity in the quality of each type, but usually, if the vendor is reliable, good materials are assured by paying a good price. Split-cane for instance is produced in a variety of grades covering a wide range of prices, but the cheaper qualities, though their cost is tempting, are generally dear in the long run. Sometimes, of course, economies can be effected by purchasing a quality of wood in accordance with the work it has to do. If its duties are such that it is not called upon to withstand severe strains, then a slightly cheaper length would be quite satisfactory ; but for fly rods, spinning rods and heavy-fish rods—in fact for all rods used for prolonged and continuous casting—the best is the cheapest in the end.

Types of Rod

The variety of fish in English waters, plus the diversity of angling methods for their capture, has created a very wide range of different types of rods. Thus for salmon we have rods for fly-fishing, spinning and trolling ; for trout, rods for wet-fly, dry-fly, dapping, spinning and bait-fishing ; for pike we have spinning and live-baiting rods ; ledgering and float-fishing rods for coarse-fishing ; and lastly, a wide variety for sea-fishing.

In addition to the main types mentioned above we have various lengths and strengths in each variety to meet the particular requirements of certain localities, or the individual peculiarities of different anglers.

With the change of angling fashions, or the advent of new ideas, new types are produced to meet the current demand. The arrival of the thread-line reel called for an entirely new type of rod which was absolutely different from the spinning rods previously used ; and now the American multiplier necessitates another change to suit its particular style of fishing.

It is impossible in a work of this length to give details for the construction of all these types, but it is also to a great extent unnecessary. The main principles of rod-building are more or less the same in every case. The chief differences lie in the length, thickness, and action of the rod, and in the materials used.

Nowadays the makers of high-class rods work on very scientific lines, and waste much valuable space in their catalogues in their endeavours to impress upon the intending purchaser the difficulties and technicalities of rod-building. The reason for all this is very obvious but it is very doubtful if all the machinery employed for calculating test-curves, breaking strains, and balance, are really necessary in the actual *making* of the rod. Statistically these figures are interesting and they no doubt help the manufacturers to arrive at a more or less standard working formula, but we venture to suggest that the amateur rod-builder can, by building the right " feel " into a rod, produce a weapon which suits his personal needs quite as well as the average shop-bought product, and at much lower cost.

" Feel " is most important in rod-building. It is a far more reliable guide than actual figures, owing to the variation in different woods. To set down a series of dimensions of rods for various purposes would result in great individual differences : no two pieces of wood are exactly alike even though they be of the same length and thickness, and outwardly bear the same appearance. This variation factor must be taken into account if the happy result is to be achieved.

Building the Rod

Let us start with a two-joint 9 ft. sea rod. For the beginner this, as a first attempt, is very suitable, for it represents one of the simplest types, does not require such precise workmanship as lighter varieties, and is robust enough to withstand any little mistakes in construction. The rod is required for pier fishing where fish of over 10 lbs. in weight are seldom encountered and the maximum weight of lead which it will be required to cast is 5 ozs.

Bearing these points in mind, and with an eye to economy, we have decided that the rod shall be of greenheart, and not too heavy.

The materials are as follows :—

Two 4 ft. 6 in. lengths of selected greenheart of suitable thickness and taper (*See* " A Few Suggested Dimensions.")

4 Intermediate rings (porcelain or agate).

1 Top ring (porcelain or agate).

1 Reinforced brass ferrule (male and female.)

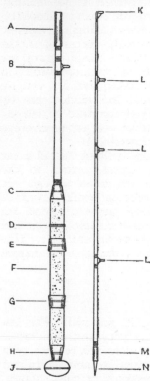

FIG. 1. ROD COMPONENTS

A = Female ferrule. B = Butt ring.   C = Top collar.   D = Retaining ring.   E = Sliding winch fitting.   F = Cork grip. G = Fixed winch fitting. H = Butt cap.   J = Rubber button. K = Top ring. L = Intermediate rings. M = Male ferrule.   N = Countersink.

1 Top collar.
1 Butt-cap.
1 Rubber button.
1 Pair winch fittings and retaining ring ($1\frac{1}{8}$ in. diam.).
2 dozen good quality corks 1 in. long and $1\frac{1}{4}$ in. diam.
1 Reel Dewhurst's Sylko (colour to taste).
1 Small tin celluloid varnish (clear).
1 Tin good copal varnish.
1 Tube of seccotine.

Some guidance as to the thickness of the wood can be obtained by consulting the graphs in the chapter entitled " A Few Suggested Dimensions." These will also be helpful in determining the inside diameter of the ferrules and top collar. Knowing that our ferrules will be fitted at a distance of $4\frac{1}{2}$ ft. from the butt end we consult the graph and find out what is the thickness of wood at this point. This, obviously, is the size of ferrule required. The same method can be applied to ascertain the size of the top collar.

The tools for rod building are simple :—

A strong-bladed knife.
A small drill.
A small tennon saw.
A few sheets of sandpaper.
A big file.
A light hammer.
Two penny paint brushes.

*   *   *   *   *

The first job is to fit the ferrules in order to get a good idea of the feel of the rod. The wood is usually supplied a little thicker than the finished product to allow for dressing-down to the requirements of the builder. To obtain the desired thickness the knife is used as a scraper.

Hold one end of the top joint in the left hand and lay the greater part of its length on a flat surface such as a table. The best position is on the edge of the table as this allows freedom of movement for the right hand. With the knife in the right hand start at the end of the wood which is farthest from the body and draw the knife evenly towards you in one long, steady, scraping stroke. This will remove a fine shaving from the entire length of the wood. Before making the next stroke the wood should be revolved very slightly with the fingers of the left hand, so that the next shaving just overlaps the first one. The process is repeated until it becomes automatic, when the rod can be shaved down with great speed.

Perhaps a few words of warning would be appropriate at this juncture. Never be in a hurry to dress the wood down—the only satisfactory method is by scraping. Greenheart cannot be successfully planed as, even with a finely-set plane, too much wood is removed with each stroke, and this causes " flats " and ovality. The grain of the wood is such that it tends to rip off in strips when the plane is used. Another point to remember is to keep each piece flat down on the table when scraping. The beginner will feel tempted to raise the left hand so that only the point rests on the table. This results in a faster cut but will cause an uneven taper due to the unequal pressure of the knife as the wood bends. Do not forget to keep the wood constantly revolving with the left hand. This will ensure that a round section is maintained throughout. Neglect of this point will cause ovality.

A very efficient scraper can be made from a small piece of broken glass. This will often perform more satisfactorily than a knife.

Scraping should be continued until the wood is reduced almost to the desired thickness. When it is apparent that it is almost small enough to suit the ferrule it should be finished off with sandpaper—first rough, then smooth. A

B

good finish having been obtained it should be revolved between the fingers to see that it is perfectly round in section.
Any oval parts or uneven tapers should be carefully
corrected.

*   *   *   *   *

Assuming that the thickness, taper, and finish are as
near right as can be decided at this stage, it is now time to
fit the male ferrule, which should be a very tight fit indeed ;
but first the builder must decide whether or not he wishes
to countersink the top joint into the butt.   A countersink
joint is a very great improvement if properly effected, and
is particularly essential on a casting rod.   It consists of a
tapered wooden extension which projects beyond the
bottom of the male ferrule, and fits into a hole of suitable
size which is bored in that part of the butt joint which is
housed in the female ferrule.   (See Fig. 2).

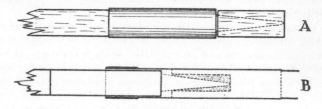

FIG. 2.   COUNTERSINKING A JOINT

A = Preparing the male end.   B = Section of finished job.
The shaded part of B is filled with wood pulp.

First the male ferrule should be fitted to the top joint
at a point 1 inch above the thick end.   To obtain a real
tight fit, the wood should have been dressed down to a
slightly greater diameter than the inside of the ferrule ;
then by judicious use of the sandpaper it is further reduced
until it will take the ferrule tightly.   Remember that the
male ferrule must fit at a point an inch above the thicker
end to allow for countersinking.   As this last inch may be
slightly thicker than the place at which the ferrule should
be, it may be necessary to slide the fitting down from the
top end of the joint.

Remember also that the male ferrule is slightly tapered and that only one end of it will fit inside the female. Make sure therefore that it is fixed in position with its thinnest end nearest the butt. Fitting of ferrules is an easy matter, but their removal, when properly fitted, is not so simple.

Occasionally, owing to a miscalculation, the rod-builder may discover that he has removed too much wood ; the result is that the ferrule is a very loose fit. When this occurs there is no need to purchase a smaller fitting. A tight binding of silk is laid on that part of the wood where the ferrule is to be fitted. This is wound on in a criss-cross fashion and is lightly smeared with Seccotine. The coils of silk are laid on until the ferrule will fit tightly over them. Some rod-builders fit all their ferrules in this way ; they claim that a ferrule so fitted is much more easily removed when circumstances necessitate a change.

To proceed with the countersinking. With a fine-cutting tennon saw make a cut around the rod immediately below the bottom end of the ferrule (Fig 2A) then proceed to shave the wood away until the tapered shape shown by the dotted line is obtained. The section of this taper should be as round as the rest of the rod ; it should be absolutely central and smoothly finished. Having got so far we shall now be obliged to leave the top joint and start work on the butt.

*   *   *   *   *

As before we have to shave down the wood until the ferrule, this time the female, can be fitted ; but first we must determine how far the wood is to be inserted into the ferrule. To decide this we make a mark on the outside of the female ferrule which indicates the distance to which its male counterpart penetrates when pushed right home. The remaining length of the female ferrule is the distance to which the top end of the butt will be inserted, less a gap of one eighth of an inch which should be left between the male ferrule and the wood of the butt (Fig. 2B). This is to allow for the gradual wear which takes place, which will ultimately result in the male ferrule sinking slightly deeper into the female. In other words the two ferrules should fit tightly by reason of the taper of the male, and not by the meeting of the two pieces of wood inside the female.

The available space in the female having been duly measured, the equivalent distance (less ⅛ inch) should be noted for the time when it is to be fitted.

The only other fitting to bear in mind at this stage is the top collar of the cork grip. Assuming that the grip is to be two feet long it is obvious that this collar must fit the wood at a point two feet from the thicker end. From here the wood tapers until an appropriate thickness occurs at the position where the ferrule is to be fitted.

For the time being then, we can afford to forget that part of the butt which is to be covered with cork so we will concentrate on the fitting of the ferrule and top collar. Thus we proceed to shave down the wood in the manner previously described until the parts fit snugly in their correct positions. The female ferrule is then removed and a hole is carefully drilled into the top end of the butt to complete the countersinking of the joint (Fig. 2B). This hole should be of just the correct width to accommodate the extension of the top joint but should be ⅛ inch deeper.

The hole is then almost filled with wood pulp or plastic wood, and the female ferrule is temporarily replaced in its correct position. Take the top joint and insert the male ferrule into the female so that it goes right home. It will thus force the tapered end into the plastic wood, and a hole will be made in the latter which will be a perfect fit for the countersunk point. Very gently and slowly the respective joints should be separated, without disturbing the plastic wood. The female ferrule can then be removed in order that any surplus filling, which has probably squeezed out, can be scraped away.

Countersinking of the joints is generally considered a very desirable feature on any rod, and the foregoing instructions show how it may be done in those cases where ordinary plain ferrules are used. A simpler procedure is to purchase ferrules on which the male is already fitted with a small extension for countersinking. In this case all that is necessary is to bore a hole in the lower joint to accommodate the extension. The extra cost of this type of ferrule is well justified.

*   *   *   *   *

The female ferrule can now be driven home to the correct distance already noted. If the wood has been properly shaved down this should be a tight driving fit.

At last the rod builder can begin to appreciate the result of his efforts, for the two joints can now be fitted together and some idea can be formed of the appearance and " feel " of the finished product.

It is a critical moment. He must now decide whether the rod will suit his purpose. Is it too heavy ? Has it sufficient action ? These are the questions he must ask himself before it is too late. If any final modifications are required they should be made now. If not, it is time to proceed with the cork grip.

*   *   *   *   *

Good quality corks can be bought with the centre-holes ready cut. These are by far the best as they are more accurate than those cut by hand. They are obtainable in a variety of sizes as regards both outside and inside dimensions. The size of hole we require is equivalent to the thickness of the rod at the point where the top collar fits. The wood below the collar should be shaved down— parallel this time, not tapered—until the corks can be pushed tightly over. To facilitate the scraping process the top collar can be temporarily removed. Corks split very easily so they should not be forced unduly. They should all be pushed into position so that the bottom end of the butt projects about two inches beyond the lowest cork.

At this stage the appearance of the grip is not very prepossessing as the irregularities in the cork give it a very uneven contour ; but this need cause no alarm for there is much trimming still to be done.

Take the tube of Seccotine and apply a liberal dose to the projecting two inches at the end of the butt. Next stand this end on the table and hold in a vertical position. Pull down the first cork until it reaches the very end and is now covering the portion to which the Seccotine was applied. In the new space thus provided a further dose of the adhesive is smeared, and the second cork is brought down *hard* on the first with as much pressure as possible. Again Seccotine is applied to the resultant gap and the third cork is brought into position. Repeat this process until every cork has been treated, and in each operation use plenty of pressure so that there are no interstices between them.

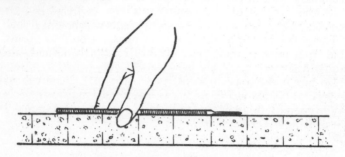

FIG. 3.   FILING THE CORK BUTT

The rod builder is now entitled to a well-earned rest which at this juncture is compulsory, for nothing more can be done until the adhesive has set and the corks are secured in their respective positions. At least twenty-four hours is necessary—forty-eight is better.

*   *   *   *   *

Now for some more trimming—this time with the file. Lay the file flat on the corks, running the same way as the butt, and proceed to move it up and down to remove the high spots (Fig. 3). It should be worked the whole length of the corks with each stroke and the rod should be slowly revolved in just the same way as when scraping the wood. Cork is very responsive to the action of a file and the grip will soon begin to look respectable.

Here again the builder should avoid the temptation to use the file in the orthodox manner (as in metal filing etc.). This is admittedly easier but will cause many irregularities.

Filing should be continued until such time as the corks are just too large to take the winch fittings. The last few corks of each end should then be tapered off until they also are just too large to admit the top and bottom collars respectively.

Next fix a sheet of rough sandpaper to a small block of

wood, and use in the same way as the file until the grip is brought a little nearer to the required thickness. Finish off with very smooth sandpaper so that the fittings can be accommodated in their final positions.

In the process of trimming down the corks it is quite possible that a few hidden cracks or faults will be unearthed. These are carefully filled with " plastic wood "—obtainable from any ironmonger—and are finally smoothed with sandpaper.

Do not make a permanent fixture of any of the fittings as yet. This should be left until the final stages. Having ascertained that each fits properly in its appointed place, these, with the exception of the top collar and the ferrules, should be removed and put in a safe place.

*   *   *   *   *

In many cases, despite the exercise of the utmost care when the wood is selected, it will be found that the assembled rod is not absolutely straight. This, however, is of little importance as the variation can be reduced to a minimum. First assemble the joints and place the butt end on eye level and look along the rod. If it is quite true, so much the better ; but if not, the individual pieces should be twisted round at the ferrule until they are united in a slightly different relative position. Again the rod can be sighted for straightness and it is quite possible that the new setting of the ferrules will have achieved the desired result. In any event it is a simple matter to rotate the top joint within the female ferrule to various positions until it has been decided which setting gives the straightest length. This should then be marked by making a scratch on the female ferrule which should coincide exactly with a similar mark on the male. Thus it is obvious that when the rod is assembled with these two marks coinciding, the alignment will be correct.

The necessity of this marking is merely temporary. It serves to set the rod in the best alignment for binding the rings into position.

Before the top ring can be fitted it is necessary to trim the tip of the rod to accommodate it. Very little advice can be given on this point owing to the variation in types

of ring.   In any case the requirements will be fairly obvious.
The ring should fit closely and the " legs " should lie on two
slightly flattened surfaces on opposite sides of the tip.   It
is thus ready for binding.

*   *   *   *   *

Now this is a tedious job for the beginner.   Before he has
proceeded far he will probably have broken several threads,
left many gaps, and have an aching wrist.   By following the
details given below, much inconvenience will be avoided
during the initiation period.   Later, when proficiency is
reached, the job is quite a pleasant one.

First let us decide the positions of the intermediate
rings.   The first or butt ring, on a rod of the type we are
making, will be fitted at a point twelve inches above the
top end of the cork grip, i.e. three feet from the bottom end
of the rod.   Mark this position clearly with a pencil and
then measure from it to a point two feet higher up the
rod.   This is the position of the second ring.   The next
two are situated at intervals of one foot ten inches and one
foot two inches respectively which results in a space of one
foot between the last mentioned ring and the tip of the rod
where, of course, the top ring is fitted.   Having marked these
points we can start to fit the top ring.

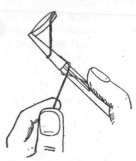

Lay it in position and secure it
temporarily with half a dozen turns
of Sylko bound round the *lower* end
of the legs.   This is to prevent the
ring from slipping during the early
stages of the binding.

The end of the thread is now held
between the fingers, and the bobbin
is placed in the left-hand pocket of
the jacket, where it will pay out
readily in response to the faintest
pull.   The thin end of the top joint
is held between the fingers of the
right hand (the butt, of course, is
removed) and the thicker end is held
between the upper arm and the body just below the right
armpit.   Now lay the thread *over* the extreme tip from the

FIG. 4A.   STARTING A
BINDING ON A ROD

left, and bring the short end round from below.   By the use
of the fingers of both hands it should be manœuvred into
the position shown in Fig 4A.

Make a few close, tight turns working downwards from
the tip.   These will secure the loose end of thread, the

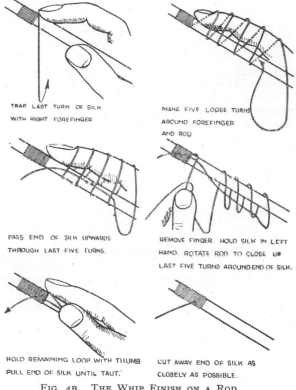

TRAP LAST TURN OF SILK
WITH RIGHT FOREFINGER

MAKE FIVE LOOSE TURNS
AROUND FOREFINGER
AND ROD

PASS END OF SILK UPWARDS
THROUGH LAST FIVE TURNS.

REMOVE FINGER. HOLD SILK IN LEFT
HAND. ROTATE ROD TO CLOSE UP
LAST FIVE TURNS AROUND END OF SILK.

HOLD REMAINING LOOP WITH THUMB
PULL END OF SILK UNTIL TAUT.

CUT AWAY END OF SILK AS
CLOSELY AS POSSIBLE.

FIG. 4B.   THE WHIP FINISH ON A ROD

surplus of which can be cut away.   Continue the binding
by revolving the top in a clockwise direction with the
fingers of the right hand.   The thread is kept tight and even
by the fingers of the left.

Each turn of thread should lie so close to its predecessor

that no gaps can be seen.   If these occur the angler should unwind the whipping until the fault is reached and then correct his mistakes.   Care should be taken to avoid straining and breaking the thread, as this will result in great waste of time and energy.

The binding of the top ring is continued until the ends of the " legs " are reached when it can be terminated by the process known as the " whip finish," which can be illustrated more clearly by the accompanying sketch than by a tedious verbal description (Fig 4B).   With regard to this finish, care should be exercised to prevent the previous coils from unwinding while the angler is engaged in finishing off.   The end of the thread is now drawn tight and cut off closely with a razor blade.   This is the process of whipping, and it does not vary whether applied to rings or to the small intermediate bindings on the rod.

*   *   *   *   *

These intermediate bindings are placed at intervals between the rings, and though they no doubt offer some measure of strength, their purpose is mainly decorative. They are placed at predetermined regular distances all along the rod, which vary between half an inch and two inches, according to the whim of the maker.   Naturally the shorter the distance the greater the number of whippings. To spare the beginner's aching wrist perhaps two inch intervals would be the wisest choice on his first home-made rod.

Starting exactly as before, but two inches below the last whipping, we lay five turns of thread, then finish off with another five thus making a complete binding of ten turns. Repeat at two inch intervals until the vicinity (previously marked) of the next ring is reached.

Lay this ring approximately in line with its brother at the top and secure temporarily with a couple of dozen turns of thread.   Then, by placing the ferrule-end to the eye and sighting along the rod, the new ring can be manœuvred until it is in perfect alignment.   Now whip as before and continue the process of whipping rings and intermediate bindings throughout the rod, not forgetting to carefully align every ring before permanently securing ;

and not forgetting also to make a half-inch whipping immediately above the male ferrule and the top collar of the cork grip, and the same below the female ferrule.

By now the amateur can begin to feel justly proud of his handiwork for the rod is approaching completion and gives a very good idea of what the finished product will look like.

* * * * *

Before continuing with the varnishing perhaps it would be as well to put the winch fittings etc. in their appointed places and to fix those which should be permanently secured.

With a very small drill, a hole should be bored in each ferrule, and in the butt cap, the lower winch fitting, and the retaining ring. The latter is the thin ring which is intended to prevent the movable winch fitting from slipping off the butt. These are then " pegged " by means of small brass sprigs (as used by shoemakers) the heads of which are trimmed away with a small file. Before pegging the lower winch fitting, which should be eight inches from the butt-end, make certain that it is in alignment with the rings. Screw the rubber button on to the butt cap.

Before the rod can be varnished with copal it is necessary that the whippings be first treated with " Cellire." Take one of the small paint brushes and apply a coat of this celluloid varnish to the first few whippings. Then, working rapidly for " Cellire " dries very quickly, hold the whipping tightly between the fingers of the left hand while the rod is revolved with the right, thus smoothing down all hairiness on the thread and forcing the varnish to soak right in. A rather sticky business but what a difference it makes.

Don't try to do too many whippings at once or you will find that the " Cellire " has become too tacky. Work in sections down the rod, and work quickly. Apply two coats to each whipping in this manner and then apply two more coats without the rubbing-in process. In each case by the time that the bottom whipping is reached, the top will be dry enough for another coat.

Leave this for a couple of hours until it is thoroughly hard and then, with the other brush apply the first coat of copal varnish. This will take about two days to become absolutely dry when a second and final coat can be applied.

The rod is now finished and will, we hope, give the builder no cause to regret the pains he has taken.

A Roach Rod

As previously mentioned, the main principles of rod-making do not vary materially ·in the production of the various types. Whether the rod be required for tunny or trout the basic ideas of construction are more or less the same, despite the wide differences in length, action, weight, and materials used. We have seen an easy method of making a greenheart sea rod, which example was chosen for its extreme simplicity ; so assuming that the reader has grasped the elementary principles underlying rod building we can go a step further. We will now make a 12-foot roach rod from Spanish Reed—a more difficult task perhaps, but one of more general interest than the previous example.

To avoid repetition of what has gone before we will abbreviate what is already known and deal mainly with the exclusive features of this particular rod.

*   *   *   *   *

First the wood. We must purchase a slightly greater length of reed than is actually required, for in the process of joining up the various thicknesses, quite a lot will be cut to waste. The chief necessity is the taper, and to ensure this we must buy about five pieces of reed which appear to be suitable for fitting consecutively one within the other, and a length of greenheart or split cane for the tip. The length of each piece may be anything up to 3 feet. This of course means that about 4 feet of wood will be wasted in the construction of a 12-foot rod, but by having a bit in hand we can select the best parts for our work and thus be assured of a really satisfactory result. If by any lucky chance the angler manages to obtain a satis-factory taper by buying fewer pieces of cane, so much the better ; but for our present purpose, we will assume the worst.

The rod is to be made in three joints. This will necessitate two pairs of ferrules, but these must not be bought until we have some idea of the size required. The other materials

are more or less the same as in the sea rod with the exception
of the rings, of which a wide variety, suitable for roach
rods, can be seen at any tackle shop. Whatever the style
of the intermediate rings, the butt and top rings should be
agate lined.

*   *   *   *   *

If the tip is included the angler now has about 18 feet
of wood out of which to make a 12-foot rod. The wood is
in six pieces, but as there are to be only two pairs of ferrules
the other pieces must be permanently united by a joint
which will be described in due course. The job of the
moment is to eliminate that material which is unnecessary
for our purpose.

Starting from the joint next to the tip, cut away each
piece of wood at a point which is most suitable for inserting
into its next-door neighbour, *but with due regard to the
fact that the total resultant length must be at least 14 feet.*
This extra 2 feet is a reserve for making the aforementioned
permanent joints. As there will be five of these joints
in all, an allowance of 4 or 5 inches is made for each one.

After cutting, lay the consecutive pieces rod-wise on the
floor, but overlap them to the extent of 4 inches at each
joint. The resultant overall length will be 12 feet, which
is thereupon divided into three equal parts, of 4 feet each.
This is done by two cuts with a tennon-saw at distances
of 4 feet and 8 feet from the butt. It is important to
remember that the ferrules will be ultimately fixed at the
points where these two saw cuts are made. All the other
joints will be countersunk by the method which we will
now describe.

*   *   *   *   *

The beginner will be wise to start countersinking at
the butt end of the rod, as the wood here is more robust
and less likely to split. By the time the delicate joints
are reached, sufficient experience will have been gained
to reduce the chances of a mishap.

The principle of countersinking is almost the same as
that of the ferrule with the exception that, instead of
metal, the natural hollowness of Spanish Reed is taken
advantage of. Another difference is that the joint we

are about to make will be a permanent fixture, and not
detachable as is the ferrule.

The inside of the higher end of the butt joint is carefully scraped out to a depth of 4 or 5 inches, the object
being that the hole provided shall accommodate the next

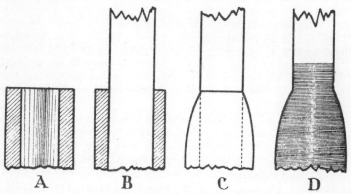

FIG. 5.   COUNTERSINKING HOLLOW CANE

consecutive piece of reed. (Fig. 5A.) The best tool for this
job is a narrow-bladed knife.   In scraping beware of using
too much pressure and consequently splitting the wood,
for Spanish Reed is very brittle.

Cease scraping as soon as the next piece can be inserted
to the required distance.   The cavity is then plentifully
daubed with glue or seccotine and the second piece driven
home.   (Fig. 5B.)   It is now allowed to set while the same
procedure is followed in the case of the other non-ferruled
joints.

We now have three pieces of wood each 4 feet long
tapering down from the thick butt to the fragile greenheart or split cane tip, but presenting a somewhat crude
appearance owing to the numerous countersunk joints
which give the rod a " stepped " effect. We will now
smooth out the " steps."

All we need is a medium file and some sandpaper, with
which we shape the wood in the fashion illustrated, taking
care not to disturb the glued joints.   (Fig. 5C.)   While
trimming we may also dress up the " knuckles " or raised

rings which appear regularly at even distances along the rod. Unlike greenheart, Spanish Reed does not have to be scraped down.

The countersunk joints are now whipped (Fig. 5D)—for safety's sake this job comes out of its turn—then the rest of the rod can be finished in the manner with which the reader is already acquainted, i.e. ferrules, cork grip, rings and whipping, then Cellire and varnish.

Do not stint the number of rings—these should be fairly close together, particularly towards the top.

A Trout Fly Rod

In the making of a fly rod there is little to add to what has gone before. The obvious differences, weight, balance, and action, are too well known to be worthy of detailed mention.

When buying the wood the builder must choose only the best quality, whether it be split-cane or greenheart. Let us take an example—a three-joint split-cane rod of 9 feet long.

Naturally the chosen wood will be as near as possible the required thickness, to avoid any unnecessary labour in reducing. The fittings will be appropriate to the particular rod in hand ; ferrules will be of the tongued type most suitable for split-cane, and preferably of the lockfast variety ; corks will be fewer as the grip need not be so long, rings will be more numerous and should be made of rustless metal in the bridge pattern.

In dressing down split cane the rod is not revolved in the same manner as for greenheart. The former is hexagonal in section and this shape must be preserved. Indiscreet revolving would soon make it round. Lay the rod on the table as before and gently scrape one surface at a time. Make certain that the action is correct before whipping on the rings.

NOTE :—There is only one correct position for a lockfast ferrule, that is, with the locking-arm lying on the opposite side to the rings when the joint is screwed home. Before fixing see that this is relatively in agreement with the predetermined position of the rings.

A Cheap Pike Rod

A pike rod, suitable for live-baiting and occasional spinning, can be màde very cheaply by using whole cane for the butt piece and greenheart for the top.

After all, the average rod of this type is seldom subjected to heavy strains as the twenty-pounders are few and far between, so a butt of cane should be capable of withstanding any normal fishing stress. We believe that the average weight of takeable pike caught in Great Britain is under five pounds. This seems to indicate that pike rods as a class are much heavier and stiffer than is actually necessary.

Whole cane is light in weight and inexpensive. It should be chosen in a thickness to blend happily with the greenheart top-joint. Best cane has a hard, polished appearance and is of a light corn colour. Straightness is absolutely essential.

No serious scraping is necessary. The only parts which require trimming are the " knuckles " or rings which appear at intervals of every few inches. These can be reduced to insignificance by the judicious use of a small file followed by a rub down with sandpaper.

Assuming that appropriate wood has been obtained the subsequent procedure is almost identical with that in the making of the sea rod. But as we are using whole cane we must remember that most of its strength lies in its hard outer shell or bark. We must therefore try to make our rod without disturbing this. In fitting the female ferrule we must choose one which gives a tight fit without making it necessary to scrape the cane to any great extent.

Proceed as before, but on reaching the whipping stage a special whipping should be made to completely cover each place from which a " knuckle " has been removed. This will correct any weakness which has been caused by the trimming.

Rings for spinning or live-baiting should be fairly large. As we require a cheap rod, porcelain linings will be more suitable than agate. The rest is simple and has already been described.

By substituting cane for greenheart on our butt joint we have saved one-third of the cost of materials.

Other Rods

The four types of rods with which we have already dealt will have given the reader a fair idea of the general procedure in amateur rod-building. With these principles in mind, plus the common sense with which all good anglers are blest, it should be an easy matter to make a rod of any desired pattern. The individual requirements of the various styles are known to most fishermen so, assuming that a decision has been made as to type, the builder has only to apply his present general knowledge to the making of the rod of his choice. If this be different from those already described, his knowledge of what is required coupled with the instructions already given, will be sufficient guide for the successful fulfilment of his project.

It is unwise to commence rod building until a decision has been made as to the exact details of the finished article, and throughout its manufacture the angler should have a clear mental picture of his objective. Some help in this direction can be obtained by trying a friend's rod. If it is suitable it can be copied as nearly as possible. The result will not be exactly the same as the original, owing to the variation in the wood, but the likeness will be near enough for all practical purposes.

Rings

When the rod has advanced to the stage at which the rings are to be fitted it will well repay the builder if he gives a little extra thought to the questions of size and number with due regard to the type of rod in hand. This is a very important point and will often make a vast difference to the rod's casting power.

Nor must we only consider casting, for the correct number and distribution of rings will help considerably in relieving the rod when under stress, and will ensure that each part of its length takes its due share of the total strain. By thus preventing any unequal stress at any point, the rings are helping to maintain that perfect straightness of rod which is so desirable.

Rings on casting rods should be as large as possible without affecting the balance. This will minimise the

C

friction between line and ring when a cast is made. The two greatest points of friction are the butt and top rings which must always be lined with porcelain or agate. The butt ring should be slightly larger than its neighbours.

*   *   *   *   *

When the rod is subjected to a working strain the tip comes in for most of the hard work, but a great deal can be done to alleviate this by correct distribution of the other rings.

It will be seen when the strain is applied, that that part of the line which runs between the reel and the top ring does not follow a curve (as the rod does) but forms rather, a series of short straight lines from ring to ring. Thus the strain is conveyed via the line to the rings and thence to the rod. The approximate share of strain which each part is bearing is indicated by the angle of each short length of line to its neighbour.

It is therefore obvious that the more rings there are, the more even will be the distribution of strain on the rod. To carry the argument further, the weaker parts (i.e. the top joint) will require more rings than the corresponding length of butt. To simplify this, the rings, which are the medium by which strain is conveyed from line to rod, should be placed at greater or lesser intervals according to the relative strengths of the various parts of the rod ; and the said intervals should be short enough to ensure the minimum of strain at each point.

FIG. 6.   RING DISTRIBUTION
A = Insufficient.   B = Correct.

In Fig. 6A we have a rod with four rings, which shows that the strain is mainly carried at these four points. The other illustration (Fig. 6B) shows the same rod with six rings, subjected to the same stress. It will be seen that in the latter the load is more evenly distributed, thus resulting in less strain-curve on the rod.

The number and distribution of rings is controlled by the strength of the rod, the purpose for which it is required, and by its length. Thus on the fragile trout fly rod we need between eight and twelve rings according to length, whereas on a sea rod five or six are usually ample. A short spinning rod will carry four or five, but a roach rod may require as many as fourteen or even more.

*   *   *   *   *

The question of the type of ring is important, though the angler cannot go far wrong in following the popular fashion. It is quite obvious that ring patterns will vary to just as great an extent as the rods themselves ; each being designed to fulfil a different purpose. On a fly rod, for instance, it is vitally necessary that weight be reduced to a minimum and, owing to the fact that the line is almost continuously in motion through the rings, it is also necessary that they should be of the " non-fouling " type. The present-day " bridge " pattern is the natural solution to the problem ; it is extremely light and does not affect the balance of the rod ; it is of such a shape that it carries the line smoothly and offers no projection which could cause a tangle.

Such a pattern is hardly suited to a roach rod, though there are many so equipped. For bottom-fishing we require a ring which will hold the wet line away from the rod, so that our cast is not retarded. A good " stand-off " pattern will do the trick.

For casting rods, as used for spinning or sea fishing, the rings should always be of the " protected " type ; an arrangement of wire around the ring prevents the vagrant line from fouling. Those most likely to foul are the butt and top rings ; if these are protected there is little risk of the line getting caught up.

" Snake " rings, which probably cost least of all, are dear at any price, and should be avoided at all costs, no matter what type of rod is being built.

False Butts

On certain types of rod a false butt is sometimes desirable. These are particularly useful on short spinning rods up to seven or eight feet, which consist of two pieces only—the butt, which is merely a grip ; and the top joint, which is a single piece of wood from the top of the grip to the top ring.

The advantage of this lies mainly in the action which the rod gives, for there is no doubt that the presence of ferrules to a certain extent robs the rod of that nicety of action and balance which we all seek. This difference has been more appreciated since the advent of the multiplier and thread-line reels, and nowadays the false-butt and single-joint are becoming increasingly popular.

The making of such a rod is in no way different from the procedure already described, except for the relative lengths of the respective pieces. 12 to 18 inches is usually long enough for the grip, and the top joint can be made to any desired length. Any kind of wood can be used as a basis for the cork grip, providing of course that it is strong and that it balances with the top.

The corks are fitted in the usual way, but for the top fitting a combined collar-cum-ferrule can be purchased which will give a better finish than could be obtained by fitting two separate units.

Another use of the false-butt is for making a combination rod, the length of which can be altered at will. Take for instance the 12 foot roach rod previously mentioned. This could be convertible from 12 feet to 10 feet simply by making a spare 2-foot false butt which fits on to the middle joint, and temporarily replaces the original 4 foot butt. To the angler who fishes different types of water this interchangeability is very useful. Multi-purpose rods are not generally in favour, but in the case of our roach rod we are merely shortening it by 2 feet to adapt it to another river.

Rod Repairs

Almost inevitably, in the course of the rod's lifetime, repairs become necessary as a result of minor accidents or carelessness. Though damage to a cherished possession is always annoying it is seldom—in the case of rods—of an irreparable nature.

Broken rings, frayed whippings and weak or distorted fittings are simple replacement operations which can easily be effected by the same methods as used in rod building.

A broken joint, however, is a more serious business, but can usually be made good by the process known as " splicing." This consists of uniting the fractured surfaces, glueing, and binding.

There are two kinds of splice. The first is the natural splice, which can only be used if the nature of the fracture is such that it presents two long tapered surfaces running at a gradual angle across the wood (Fig. 7A). The surfaces should be generously glued and then brought together so that they fit in exactly the same manner as before they

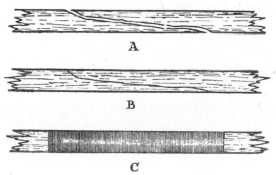

A

B

C

FIG. 7. REPAIRING A NATURAL SPLICE

were broken (Fig. 7B). A rough but tight whipping is then applied to keep them in position until the glue is set. This takes two or three days (the longer the better), and throughout this period the rod must lay flat on a horizontal surface. Do not lean it against a wall as this will probably cause a bend at the weakened part.

When the glue is set the whipping can be carefully removed and the surplus glue sand-papered away. Start the final whipping at a point half an inch above the upper end of the splice and continue until the entire break is

covered plus an additional half-inch below the lower end.
This whipping should be as tight as possible (Fig. 7C).

The surrounding varnish will have been previously
removed to facilitate the process, so now the whipping is
treated with Cellire. When this is dry the rod is finished
with the appropriate exterior varnish.

*   *   *   *   *

Unfortunately many of the breaks which occur do not
lend themselves to repairing by the " natural splice "
method. These are what may be called " short breaks "
which run almost at right-angles to the grain as if the wood
had been sawed. Obviously the exposed fractured surfaces
are much too small to hold together with glue and whipping,
so it is necessary to elongate them by shaving down each
piece to the desired angle. This is rather a tricky business,
requiring great care and patience.

First, by the use of a sharp chisel, cut away the wood to
approximately the correct angle, and by placing the two
pieces together see that these result in a piece which is
more or less straight. If the angles are not identical in
each case a bend will be apparent which must be rectified
before proceeding.

Now fasten a piece of fine sandpaper on a perfectly flat
top of a table. Lay each splice surface in turn on this and
move gently to and fro until it is perfectly true and flat

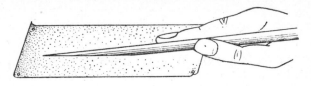

FIG. 8.   SANDPAPERING SURFACE FOR SPLICING

(Fig 8). If this is done correctly it should result in two
identical surfaces which when fitted together will form an
absolutely straight rod which can now be glued, whipped,
and varnished.

*   *   *   *   *

A common form of damage to rods is the bending or warping of the wood due either to strain or to imperfections in the material used. Sometimes bends occur in the ferrules, but these are easily remedied by replacing the weakened fitting. Most bends, however, are the result of fishing or casting stresses and cause the rod to be strained in a sideways or downwards direction—generally the latter.

Let us assume that a rod has become bent in a downwards direction as a result of fishing strains (big fish, we hope). (Fig 9A.) The cause of the damage can be employed to effect the cure. All we have to do is to remove the rings

FIG. 9. STRAIGHTENING BENT JOINTS
A = Joint bent downwards. B = Rings reversed.

and whip them on the *opposite* side of the rod, which will then have an upward curve, for the top side of the rod has now become the bottom (Fig 9B). This upward curve will presumably be subjected to similar strains, which will in course of time pull down the curve until the rod is straight again.

Distortion due to the casting of heavy lures can be reduced in the same way even though the deviation be sideways rather than downwards. The reversal of the rings causes the new strain to correct the effects of the old.

* * * * *

A rod should always be kept well varnished. This is its only protection from damp and subsequent rotting. If in the course of use the varnish becomes chipped or scratched these places should be filled in with a dab from a small brush. Every year a good coat must be applied and special attention should be paid to the places where the wood is enclosed within ferrules, etc., as damp often penetrates the

interstices between wood and metal.   The area around the
ring whippings is also worthy of attention, for this is another
holding place for moisture.   Before varnishing, be certain
that the wood is absolutely dry.

Accidents to rods can be avoided only by the exercise
of care and common sense.   A good angler should take the
same precautions in the use of his rod as a good shooter
does with his gun.   Watch a good shooter when the
opportunity arises.   Note how carefully he carries his
weapon ;   note his precautions when negotiating ditches,
stiles or fences ;   note his care in selecting a spot to lay it
down.   These are the things which prevent accidents and
damage.   In shooting they are unwritten rules, but in
angling they are left to the discretion of the fisherman.

A Few Suggested Dimensions

We offer below, for the guidance of the beginner, a few
approximate thicknesses of greenheart and split-cane as
used in various types of rods.   This may be of some help
in deciding thickness and taper when ordering rod timber.

We are fully aware, in presenting these figures, of the
serious discrepancies which may occur as the result of the
variations in different pieces of wood.   This variation factor
has already been mentioned and it is hoped that the reader
will appreciate the fact that the figures can only be given
as a rough guide.   They are intended to be of service to the
man who is uncertain as to the proportions of rods used for
various purposes.   If he uses this information in laying the
foundation of his rod he can make final alterations, so that
it " feels " right, afterwards.   It is best to err on the safe
side :   a slight surplus of wood can easily be removed, but
it is impossible to make a thin joint thicker.

There is also the question of taste to be considered in
regard to the action of a rod.   The dimensions given may
be quite suitable to some anglers, and useless to others.
Likewise, the rod which is suitable for catching nine-inch
brook trout would not be " man " enough to deal with the
giants of the Hampshire chalk streams.   Bearing all this
in mind the reader must consider the following figures with
reserve.

*   *   *   *   *

For the sake of simplicity the measurements are given in the form of graphs. The figures along the top of the

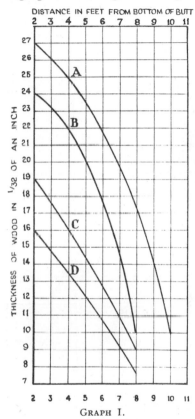

GRAPH I.

This graph shows the tapers of four different sea rods. Type A is a powerful 10-foot weapon suitable for heavy casting from the beach.   Type B is also a heavy rod capable of handling almost any fish in British waters, but it is two feet shorter than A.   It is a very suitable rod for boat fishing.

Type C is a much lighter rod though capable of handling heavy fish. It is a good all-rounder for the angler who fishes for heavy fish with fairly light tackle.

Type D is an ultra light rod for sea fishing.   It will cast leads up to three ounces, but must be used with discretion.   It is an ideal rod for float fishing or light trolling. Variations between A and D, both in length and thickness, will provide a wide range of rods suitable for all classes of sea fishing.

graph represent the distance in feet from the extreme end of the butt. It will be noticed that the first reading is taken at a point two feet from the butt end.

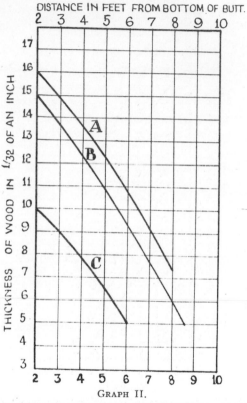

DISTANCE IN FEET FROM BOTTOM OF BUTT.

GRAPH II.

This graph shows three spinning rods suitable for salmon or pike. Type A is an eight-footer made for heavy casting, an ideal rod for fishing flooded water. It would also make a good live-bait rod for pike. Type B is much lighter and slightly longer; it has a much softer action. Nevertheless, it is capable of holding a heavy fish. Type C is a light, stiff, six-foot rod suitable for use with a fixed-spool reel or multiplier.

The figures down the left hand side of the graph represent the thickness of the wood in units of one thirty-secondths of an inch. In Graph 1 for instance the scale of thicknesses ranges from $\frac{27}{32}$ in. down to $\frac{7}{32}$ in.

Line A in Graph I represents a heavy sea rod of ten feet long. It will be seen from the graph that the thickness of wood at a point two feet above the end of the butt is $\frac{27}{32}$ in., and that the rod tapers down to $\frac{10}{32}$ in. $(\frac{5}{16})$ at the

DISTANCE IN FEET FROM BOTTOM OF BUTT

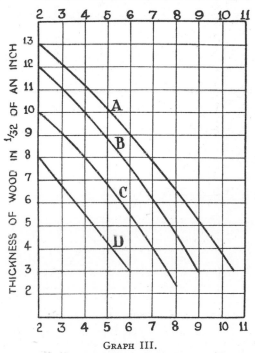

GRAPH III.

Here we have four trout-fly rods. Once again A is the most powerful. a 10-feet 6-inch weapon suitable for loch fishing or for heavy quarry. At a pinch it would do for grilse. B is also quite a sturdy rod, but is only nine feet in length. C is eight feet long and much lighter. D is essentially a brook rod, six feet long ; just the rod for fishing well-bushed streams.

tip. These figures could have been given without having recourse to a graph ; but the advantage is that the graph also shows the *intermediate* thickness at any given point.

Thus we see that at three feet the rod has decreased to $\frac{26}{32}$ in. ; at four feet to $\frac{25}{32}$ in. ; at eight feet to $\frac{17}{32}$ in ; and so on. The unit figure is $\frac{1}{32}$ of an inch in each case ; it can easily be converted to sixteenths or eighths according to the numerator figure.

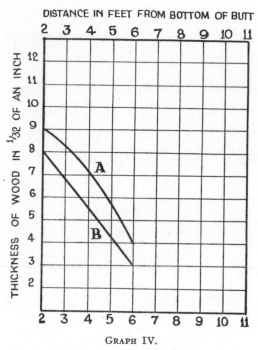

GRAPH IV.

These are two trout spinning rods. Type A is light but sufficiently powerful to handle large fish. Type B is lighter still and is hardly strong enough to deal with fish of more than average weight. Both are essentially designed for use with a threadline reel.

All you have to do is to run down the vertical line (the distance in feet) to the point where the rod-line (A, B, C, or D) crosses. Read horizontally to the left from this point and you can ascertain the precise thickness of the wood at any given distance from the butt.

II

SPINNING TACKLES

No matter whether the angler spins for salmon, trout, pike or sea fish, he can make quite a useful variety of dead-bait spinners at a negligible cost. This is a great advantage to spinning men, for in their branch of the sport much tackle is lost on bushes and submerged snags. If the lost tackles be of the shop-bought variety a day's spinning can become a very expensive business.

The varieties of dead bait tackles are legion but can be roughly divided into two main classes—those which cause the bait to spin while it is retrieved, and those which merely produce a wobble. The former are fitted with a propeller vane which causes rotation, whereas the latter have none, but are so designed that the bait can be mounted to produce the wobble effect.

These two main classes can be sub-divided into others too numerous to mention. Great variety is necessary owing to the diversity in the sizes and shapes of baits. Such widely assorted types as minnows, sand eels, and prawns obviously call for individual treatment. Apart from the necessity of making tackles of various sizes in proportion to the size of the bait, there is also the question of security to be considered. Owing to anatomical differences of the lures used, it is impossible to design a universal standard mount.

*　　　*　　　*　　　*　　　*

The materials used in making spinning tackles are very simple and are useful in other branches of tackle making. The first essential is a spool of fine silk for binding the hooks to gut ; any neutral colour will suit. All silk should be well waxed before use ; cobbler's wax is best for this purpose, and can either be applied dry or in liquid form.

The latter procedure is more effective and is described in the chapter on " Hook Tackles."

Celluloid or shellac varnish, for applying to the finished binding, is also essential. The former, though dearer, is preferable. An inexpensive substitute can be made up by the formula mentioned in " Hook Tackles " ; this is not so good as the shop-bought product, mainly because it lacks body, but it is just as effective if a few extra coats are applied. The extra applications do not entail any particular inconvenience because the varnish dries in a few minutes.

A small vice, as used for fly-dressing, is a great asset, particularly when dealing with the smaller tackles.

Minnow-Fishing Tackles

Starting with the wobble tackles, perhaps the simplest of all is that illustrated in Fig. 10. This consists of three trebles size 16 to 14, a small mouth lead, a tiny swivel, and a length of gut of gauge ½x drawn. A reel of binding silk, some cobbler's wax, and a tin of celluloid varnish are required for binding the trebles to gut.

The mouth lead is made from thin lead wire. A short length of the wire is bent into the shape shown in Fig. 10A, and the main length is then coiled closely around the centre stem until the coil is about an inch long (more for larger tackles). The ends of wire are then trimmed away and the mouth lead is sharpened to a point. A coat of celluloid varnish will be of great help in holding the coils in position.

Next take the piece of gut, and to it join another short piece using the knot shown in Fig. 15G. The respective lengths are indicated in Fig. 10B. Bend back the last half-inch of the longer piece of gut and lay the treble into the bend as shown. With well-waxed silk whip along the shank of the treble, thus securing the hook.

Another treble is bound to the same piece of gut at a distance of three-quarters of an inch from the first. The gut cannot be doubled back as it was for the first hook, so care must be taken to whip it very tightly.

Before binding in the third treble it is necessary to thread the gut into position through the eye of the mouth lead.

This is done by a " cross-over " method as shown.   The last hook can then be bound to the other strand of gut, after which the whippings should be given a generous coat of celluloid varnish.

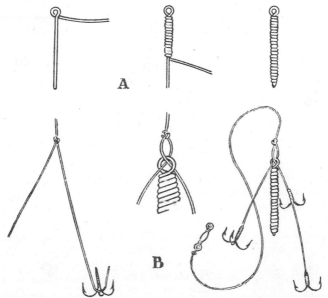

FIG. 10.   A NEAT " WOBBLE " TACKLE FOR MINNOW FISHING

Personally we often use fine plated copper wire for binding small trebles to gut.   It is more manageable than silk and saves a lot of time.   It is doubtful if it will last as long, but in our experience most spinning tackles are lost on snags long before their useful span of life is ended.   Why then should we go to the trouble of building a long-lived tackle when in all probability it will be lost during its first day's use ?

The lengths of the hook-carrying pieces of gut in this tackle are subject to slight variations to suit the size of minnow used.   The lengths shown represent a fair average.

*   *   *   *   *

Another simple " wobble " tackle for minnows can be made by using a prong of brass wire to replace the lead. Take a small swivel and a 6 inch length of brass wire

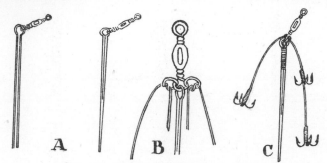

FIG. 11.   ANOTHER " WOBBLE " TACKLE

(gauge 20 or 21).   Pass the swivel half way along the wire and then bend into the shape illustrated in Fig. 11A. The spike should now be cut down to 1½ inches long and

a smear of solder is run between the " legs."   File the end to a sharp point to assist penetration.   Bind on three treble hooks as in the previous pattern and attach the two gut-ends to the lower eye of the swivel by means of half-hitches (Fig. 11B).   Pull the knots close, but not tight, and bind the loose ends to the centre spear.   Finish the binding with a coat of varnish. (Fig. 11C.)

When in use this spear can be bent to almost any shape to produce various degrees of wobble.   If it is considered desirable to add a little extra weight this can be done by coiling a length of thin lead wire along the spike close up to the swivel.   The ingoing end of the lead should be tapered down to facilitate insertion. (Fig. 12.)

FIG. 12.   AS FIG. 11, BUT FITTED WITH MOUTH LEAD AND EXTRA HOOK

*   *   *   *   *

A small tackle of the Dee type is favoured by some anglers for minnow fishing. It is quite a good type but does not hold the bait so securely as the style of mount illustrated in Fig. 10. Two No. 14 trebles are bound to $\frac{1}{2}$x drawn gut at a distance of about $1\frac{1}{4}$ inches apart. The main length of gut is then passed through the eye of a small lead and the tackle is ready for use. (Fig. 13.)

FIG. 13.   DEE TACKLE

Occasionally a very small mouth lead is required for use with tiny minnows. The coil type previously mentioned would be too bulky for this purpose, in which case it may be necessary to purchase a supply of the type similar to those used in the " Aerial " tackle.

The only other " wobble " flights in general use consist of a row of two or three trebles mounted on gut with an adjustable lip hook slightly above. This pattern has many bad points and has been almost superseded by those already described. They carry no weight except on the trace ; they have a very indifferent grip of the bait and after a few casts the hooks begin to tear away.

*   *   *   *   *

We can now pass from the subject of " wobbling " tackles to deal with the almost inexhaustible variety of spinners. These are so numerous that it is impossible to deal with every pattern, particularly as many of the differences are almost insignificant. We are concerned only with those types which can be made at home with the use of inexpensive materials. Any angler of an inventive turn of mind can, from the main patterns given, produce variations to suit his fancy.

All true spinning tackles embody in their design some sort of propeller to produce a revolving movement when water resistance is felt. In shop-bought products these vanes are either of metal or celluloid. For the amateur tackle maker the latter is infinitely superior, though occasionally metal has its uses. We are of the opinion that celluloid is also better from the angling point of view, being almost invisible in the water and immune from corrosion or rot.

The best all-round thickness is $\frac{1}{32}$ of an inch. It should be fresh stock, not old and brittle. A shilling or less, spent with a coach builder, will provide sufficient to make a good supply of tackles.

With a pair of strong scissors cut from the celluloid a sufficient number of propellers of the shape shown in Fig. 14A. For minnow fishing the overall width should not exceed one inch. Now take eight inches of gauge 21 or 22 brass or copper wire. This is a greater length than is actually required but the extra makes for easier handling

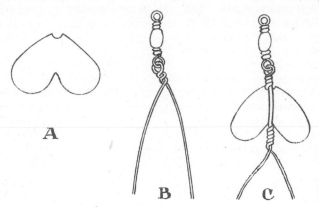

FIG. 14.   FITTING A PROPELLER

and can be cut away afterwards. Make a very small loop in the middle of the wire and slide a swivel into this position. Twist *both* wires together for three turns, thus securing the swivel (Fig. 14B). Place one of the propellers close up to the last twist, bring down the wires flat against the propeller, one each side, and recommence twisting so that this also is secured. (Fig. 14C.) Cut off the wire leaving a total length, excluding swivel, not exceeding two inches. Run a little solder along the wire so that the whole is held tightly, and file the end to a point.

Put the lot in boiling water to prepare the celluloid for bending, meanwhile a pair of round-jawed pliers (as described in " Wirework ") can be heated over a gas ring. If cold pliers are used they will instantly nullify the effect of the hot water.

As soon as the celluloid is pliable bend the vanes round in opposite directions so that the mean angle between them is a little less than 90°. Place in cold water to set.

The only remaining job is to fix the flight of hooks, and it is here that the angler can indulge his fancy as to number and type. Two or three hooks can be used—either small trebles or large singles. The favourite mount is three trebles size 14, two on one side and one on the other.

Whip the first two within an inch of each other on the gut, pass the free end of gut through the eye of the swivel and fasten with a half-hitch. The other treble can now be whipped to the remaining end. Varnish the whippings and the tackle is complete (Fig. 15).

FIG. 15.
REVOLVING
MINNOW
TACKLE

If the angler requires a slightly heavier spinner he can wind a close coil of thin lead around the spike, starting immediately below the propeller and working downwards. As usual the penetrating end of this coil should be tapered.

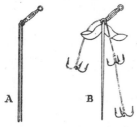

FIG. 16. ANOTHER
REVOLVING TACKLE

*　　*　　*　　*

A similar tackle can be made without the necessity of twisting the wire.

Cut the celluloid as before, but use a $3\frac{1}{2}$ in. length of gauge 20 wire. Fold the wire over double so that it represents an attenuated letter U, and pass a swivel up to the bend (Fig. 16A). Pinch the two " legs " of wire close together throughout their entire length which is now $1\frac{3}{4}$ inches.

Slide a propeller into position close up to the top end.
Solder the two " legs " together from below the propeller
to the point.   Sharpen the end with a small file.   The vanes
can be bent, and the hooks mounted, in the manner previously described (Fig. 16B).

*   *   *   *   *

Where celluloid is used the propellers are held solely by
the grip of the wires, whereas if the vanes be of a non-
corrosive metal the grip can be
reinforced by the application of a
little solder and a neater and
stronger tackle will result.

To make a good metal-vaned
spinner cut out the propeller in the
requisite shape and trim up all
rough edges—these are dangerous
as they may chafe the gut.   Double
back the last half-inch of a fairly
stout piece of wire and slide a
swivel into the bend (Fig. 17A).
Place the propeller in the clip thus
formed and pinch tightly with pliers.   Solder the wire into
position on both sides of the vane and attach the hooks in
the usual way.   Sharpen the spike to a point and add lead
wire if desired (Fig. 17B).

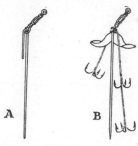

A   B

FIG. 17.   REVOLVING TACKLE
WITH METAL VANE

Spinning Tackles for Larger Baits

Such baits as sand-eels, sprats, gudgeon, roach, etc., as
used by salmon and pike anglers will obviously require
more powerful tackles than those used for minnows.
Propellers must be larger to spin the heavier lure.   Trebles
are larger, and in some cases of a different pattern.   In
many instances gut is replaced by wire or gimp.

Once again we are able to choose between " wobbling "
and spinning patterns.   The most popular of the former
is the Dee type.   Apart from its size it varies but little
from the pattern described for trout, the chief difference
being that for larger fish it is usual to thread the mount
through the vent of the bait and bring it out through his

mouth. The lead is then threaded on and is also pushed into the mouth.

This pattern is unsuitable for fragile thin-bodied fish such as sprats or sand-eels but is quiet satisfactory for roach, gudgeon, etc.

The size of treble depends entirely on the size of the bait. For smaller fish such as gudgeon a number six or seven would be large enough, but a number three or two would be required when using a roach or herring. Strong salmon gut is best for mounting salmon tackles, but if pike are the quarry the mount should be on fine wire or gimp. Either can be used double if so desired.

A strong tackle can be made by bending a piece of wire or gimp into the fashion shown in Fig. 18A and inserting two appropriate sized trebles in the positions indicated (B). Whip as shown with strong thread and then apply varnish.

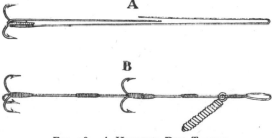

FIG. 18.   A HEAVIER DEE TACKLE

The whipping is finished off at about an inch from the penetration end. A loop is thus formed for attaching the cast. If the angler so desires the hooks can be of the double type with the side spike for securing the bait.

*   *   *   *   *

Another wobble tackle which offers greater security than the Dee type can be made along the same lines as the second of the minnow tackles (Fig. 11) but the component parts should be increased in size and strength to deal with the larger baits. The spike or spear should be 2 inches to $3\frac{1}{2}$ inches long; the trebles size seven to two; and the mount, of strong salmon gut or flexible wire.

Simplicity is a very desirable feature in all spinning tackles, especially if it incorporates invisibility and strength. For this reason we are inclined to favour the tackle shown in Fig. 19.

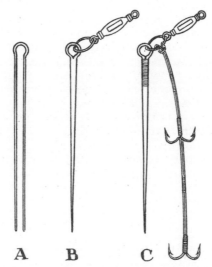

FIG. 19. " WOBBLE " TACKLE FOR LARGE BAITS
(Note split ring for hook flight attachment.)

The component parts are a swivel, a split ring, a length of thin brass or copper wire, two trebles, and a strand of strong salmon gut or good gut substitute.

Double the gut in the same manner as shown in Fig. 18A, and bind two suitable-sized trebles into position. The end treble should lie *inside* the loop of the gut so that its security is doubled, i.e. it is held by the whipping and by the loop, and cannot be pulled out of the former unless the latter breaks. The same applies to the second treble which lies in the bend of the short length of gut which is doubled back. When the whole lot is whipped tightly to the shank of the hook it cannot be separated by any normal fishing strain.

Bend a piece of gauge 20 brass or copper wire into the shape shown in Fig. 19A. Fix the split ring to one eye of the swivel and pass the wire through the split ring until the latter lies in the loop at the top of the wire (Fig. 19B). Solder the two legs of wire together, and for extra security whip the first half-inch below the top loop. Sharpen the other end to a point.

If the angler is not keen on soldering—some people fight shy of this job—he should first sharpen the legs to a point and then whip, with strong thread or fine copper wire, from the top loop downwards to within half an inch of the sharpened end. This whipping should be well varnished. The result is not so satisfactory as soldering but will give reasonably good service.

Pass the loop of the gut through the split ring, open it out and pass the hooks through, then pull the gut fairly tight. (Fig. 19C).

Owing to the fact that this pattern does not in any way mutilate the bait, it can be used on the more delicate varieties such as sand eels and sprats providing that variations are made in length and hook size to suit the fish in use.

Another way of making the body spear of this tackle is as follows. Take the necessary length of brass wire (gauge

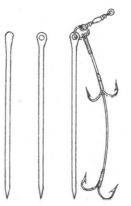

FIG. 19D. As FIG. 19, BUT USING THICK SINGLE WIRE FOR BODY SPEAR

14 this time) and hammer one end flat as shown in Fig. 19D; the other end is sharpened to a point. A very small hole is drilled through the flattened end and into this the split-ring is inserted. The rest of the procedure is exactly the same as in the previously mentioned tackle. This type of body spear is worth remembering ; it can be used in many cases instead of twisted or soldered wire, and is very simple to make.

*   *   *   *   *

Now for the revolving patterns. Celluloid is again an easy favourite for making propellers but these will need to be larger than those recommended for minnows. Nevertheless the tackle recommended for the smaller fish and illustrated in Fig. 15 will also be very suitable for larger fish providing that suitable increases are made in size and strength. When finished the tackle can be leaded or left unleaded as desired.

Then there is the other pattern illustrated in Fig. 16. This is the type in which the wires of the spear are not twisted together but are secured by solder only. It also is quite suitable for larger baits.

The total width of the celluloid vanes must be increased to between $1\frac{1}{2}$ inches and 2 inches, and the depth from $\frac{1}{2}$ inch to almost an inch. The length of the spear (below the propeller) should be about $2\frac{1}{4}$ inches for medium sized baits but can be increased to 4 inches for roach, sand eels, etc. Trebles range in size from sevens to twos.

While speaking of roach perhaps it is necessary to mention that these deep-bodied fish offer a fair amount of resistance to water, and tend to obstruct the propeller in its work. Also there is a possibility of the propeller turning a little faster than its slow-moving burden. Thus the tackle may twist slightly inside the bait which will result in insecurity.

The outcome of this is that " wobble " tackles are superior to revolving tackles for deep bodied fish unless some added security can be obtained by a slight alteration of pattern. In this connection the angler will find a few suggestions at the end of this chapter in the section entitled " A few variations." This section is intended to help him to indulge any personal fancies he may have.

Any ideas contained therein can be applied to what has already been written about spinning tackles, with the result that the reader will be able to make almost any of the simple types. There are certain shop patterns of course, which are very complicated pieces of ironmongery produced by special machinery. The amateur tackle maker is advised to leave these alone and to satisfy himself with plain easy-to-make types.

Prawn Tackles

It is possible that more ingenuity has been expended over prawn tackles than over any other type. The reason for this is obvious. Prawns are a very fragile bait which must be held securely by a tackle which does not mutilate them. They are also comparatively small and should not alarm the fish by being encased in too much ironmongery. Then again, they are usually used when rivers are low and clear, when fish are abnormally shy, a further demand for a light and invisible outfit.

The prawn himself offers us no help whatever in our search for the perfect tackle. Most unobligingly he has a very small mouth into which no weight can be inserted. Thus lead must be added to the exterior decorations.

Despite all these drawbacks it is possible for the amateur to make several reliable patterns.

*　　　*　　　*　　　*　　　*

A delightfully simple design is illustrated in Fig. 20, and consists of a wire spear, a strand of good salmon gut, a double hook with side spike, a treble hook, and some thin lead wire.

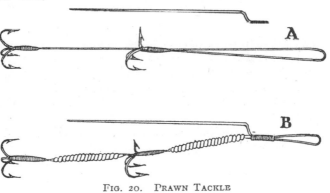

FIG. 20. PRAWN TACKLE
(Note lead wire above hook shanks.)

Sharpen the spear to a point (we recommend rustless steel gauge 20 in this case). The length may be anything between two and three inches according to the size of the prawn. The hooks, which may be of any size between 10 and 6, are bound to the doubled gut with waxed thread, at a distance of about 1½ inches apart. If desired an extra double hook can be added on the larger editions of this

tackle, and should be bound on slightly above. Lay the
blunt end of the spear, which should be free from roughness
or sharp edges, into position half an inch below the upper
loop formed by the doubled gut, and secure the gut to wire
with a binding not exceeding a quarter of an inch in length.
Wind two close coils of thin lead wire around the gut
immediately above the hook shanks. The lead can be
painted a dirty pink or light brown colour to match the
prawn.

This tackle does not embody a swivel in its design.
From the spinning point of view this is unnecessary as
the bait does not revolve. Some anglers favour swivels
even on non-revolving baits and argue that these are
justified in view of the possibility of the fish twisting the
cast. This is a very remote possibility and is just as
unlikely in prawn spinning as it is in fly fishing. As far
as possible therefore, we will omit this accessory from
tackles of the non-revolving type. The angler who prefers
them can insert them in the loop made for cast attachment.

*   *   *   *   *

A secure pattern can be made as follows. Take a piece
of gauge 20 rustless wire of two to three inches long, and

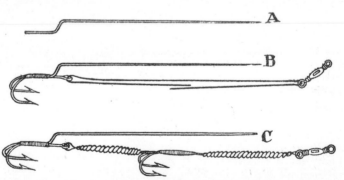

FIG. 21.   PRAWN TACKLE.   ANOTHER WAY OF MOUNTING THE
BODY SPEAR

sharpen one end to a point. Then bend as shown in Fig. 21A.
Lay this on the shank of a size 4 double hook and whip

securely with wire or strong waxed thread. Bend another
length of thin rustless trace wire into the shape shown
and commence binding along the wire with strong thread.
At approximately $1\frac{1}{2}$ inches from the tail hook another of
the same size should be bound in, after which the binding
should be continued to the swivel at the head. After
varnishing the binding, a thin coil of lead wire should be
added to give the necessary weight. Paint the lead to
imitate the roe of the prawn. When in use the spear is
inserted at the head of the prawn and passed through the
body towards the tail. A few turns of silk should then be
wound around the tail to hold it closely to the exterior
wire.

*   *   *   *   *

It is quite an easy matter to make adjustable prawn
tackles. On these the spear is usually eyed at the head
in such a fashion that the gut which carries the hooks can
slide up or down according to the
size of the bait. A simple form
is illustrated in Fig. 22.

Take three inches of gauge 20 wire
and bend as in Fig. 22A. Whip just
below the eye so that the short
leg is secured to its longer neighbour. Sharpen the end of the long
wire. Whip two double or treble
hooks to a length of stout salmon
gut, pass this through the eye and
loop the other end for attachment
to the trace. (Fig. 22B.) Do not
forget that when attaching the
bottom hook the last half inch of
wire should be passed between the
hooks of the treble and doubled

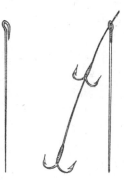

A   B
FIG. 22.   ADJUSTABLE
PRAWN TACKLE

back along the shank. Thus when whipped it is doubly
secured.

*   *   *   *   *

The eye at the head of the spear can be produced in
another way. Fold one inch of gut substitute into a thin
letter U. Bind this on to an absolutely plain spear as

shown in Fig. 23A. A very small loop should be left at the head so that the hook-gut can be passed through (Fig. 23B).

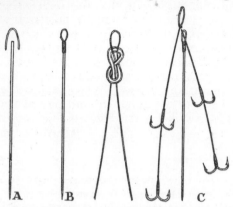

FIG. 23. ADJUSTABLE PRAWN TACKLE FOR LARGE BAITS

Thus we have our spear with a flexible eye. We will embody this in our next tackle.

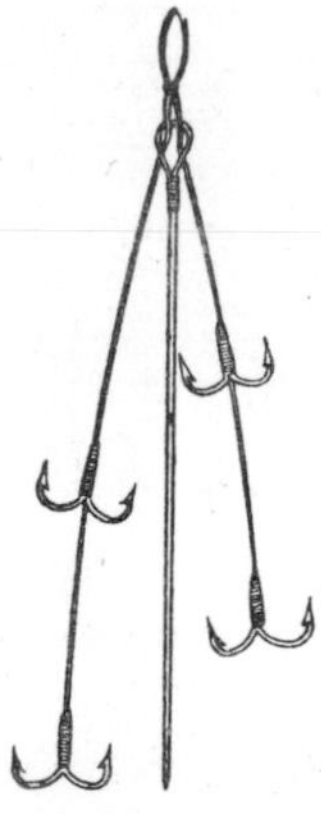

Having made the spear we knot a piece of gut into the pattern illustrated either adding or omitting a swivel according to taste. Thread one length of gut through the eye of the spear and whip on two trebles at a distance of 1½ inches apart. Now whip either one or two trebles to the free length of gut and the tackle should look something like Fig. 23C.

Should the angler prefer it, both hook-lengths of gut can be made to pass through the eye. This effect is shown in Fig. 24.

FIG. 24.
A VARIATION OF
FIG. 23

*   *   *   *

A very secure prawn tackle is illustrated in Fig. 25. A spear is made from rustless steel wire (gauge 20) and is sharpened to a point at one end. At about a quarter of an inch above the point the wire is bent into the shape shown in Fig. 25A. At the other end of the wire a short length of strong springy gut-substitute is bound, and this should be varnished with " Cellire " in order that it will not become limp when in water. An inch length of brass or copper

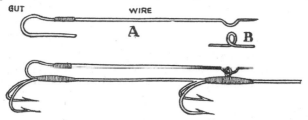

FIG. 25. A VERY SECURE PRAWN TACKLE

wire (gauge 24) is bent into the shape B. and is bound to the foremost of the hooks as shown in the sketch. The other end of the gut " spring " is bound to the shank of the tail hook. The bindings are then varnished.

In practice the spear is passed through the prawn until the point projects about half an inch. Then, easing the wire back on the gut spring, the point is passed into the tiny eye on the foremost hook ; the kink in the wire will quickly fall into position in the eye, thus securing the bait.

* * *

The first of the revolving tackles is very similar to one of those previously de-scribed for minnows. There is one notable difference

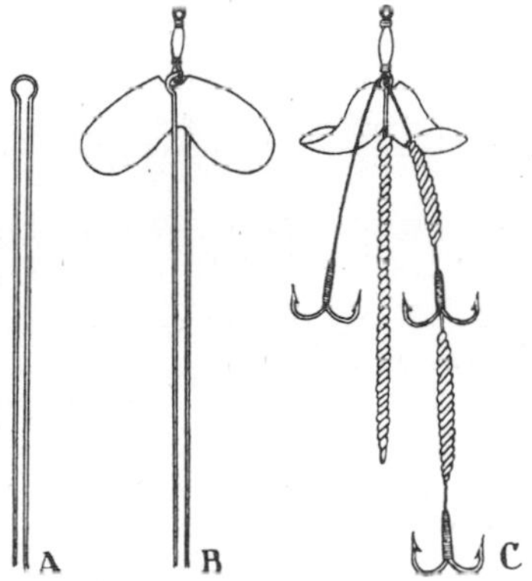

FIG. 26. REVOLVING PRAWN TACKLE
Note lead wire above hooks

however, in that the lead is carried on the hook length of gut instead of on the spear.

Cut a piece of celluloid of the shape illustrated in Fig. 14A, having an outside total width of 1 inch to 1½ inches. Bend an 8 inch length of wire into the shape of a split pin, i.e. legs together and loop at top (Fig. 26A) ; pass a swivel into the

loop, push up the propeller, and then twist the remaining
length of wire to form a spear. Mount the hooks as previously described for the minnow tackle illustrated in
Fig. 15. Coil lead wire just above the hook shanks.

*   *   *   *   *

For small prawns a tackle equipped with a single treble
hook is sometimes preferable. The type illustrated in
Fig. 27 suits the purpose very well. Cut a small propeller

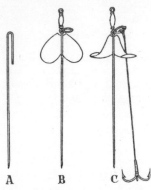

of the usual shape and insert
it in the bend of a piece of
rustless steel wire shaped as
in sketch, after ·first fitting a
swivel therein. Bind the two
wires together immediately
below the celluloid vane
(Fig. 27B).

Work the split ring on to
the lower eye of the swivel,
and to this attach the looped
gut which carries the treble.
The length of the hook flight
should very slightly exceed
the length of the spear. The
result is a very neat tackle.

A   B   C

FIG. 27.   FOR SMALL PRAWNS
AND SHRIMPS

If extra weight is required it should be added, in the form
of lead wire, to the gut, after which it should be painted a
suitable colour to match the prawn.

*   *   *   *   *

Great security can be ensured by a tackle on which the
spear is reversed, i.e. the point faces the direction to which
the bait is travelling.

This body spear, made of rustless steel wire, is of the
same shape as shown in Fig. 20A, and is bound to the shank
of a treble hook of size 5 or 6. Another length of slightly
thinner wire (say gauge 21) is attached by a loop (see
" Wirework," Fig. 114) to the eye of the hook, and the
remaining length is bent round as shown in Fig. 28A. First
a swivel, and then a celluloid propeller, are placed in position

in the bend of the wire and the end is brought down and twisted around the lower end of the vane. Propeller and swivel are thus securely held in place. The finished tackle is shown in Fig. 28. If desired, an extra hook and body lead can be added as shown in the next sketch.

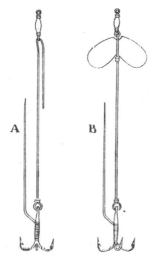

FIG. 28. SECURE REVOLVING TACKLE FOR PRAWNS

FIG. 29. AS FIG. 28 BUT FITTED WITH LEAD BODY AND EXTRA HOOK

Unfortunately it is not always possible to use rustless steel wire as a body spear. This metal cannot be soldered and is therefore unsuitable for those tackles where the propeller is held between soldered wires. But wherever possible it should be used in preference to brass, to which it is infinitely superior. These remarks apply only to its use as a body spear as shown in Figs. 20 to 25 and 27 and 28 ; in other cases, where brass is specified, it is more suitable than rustless steel.

A Few Variations.

In the foregoing patterns of spinning tackles we have mainly used the treble hook. This is deservedly the most popular and is undoubtedly the most generally useful, but anglers differ widely in their choice of equipment so perhaps a few words should be said of other types.

Single hooks, for instance, are advocated by some anglers of great experience. The hook should be slightly larger than the treble and must be fixed so that it stands well clear of the bait to effect certain penetration. The main advantages of single hooks are their unobtrusiveness and the fact that they are much less likely to get caught up. A few anglers claim that they have greater hooking power, but this seems hardly likely.

Double hooks are very neat and lie closely to the bait, but they have no holding power on the latter unless they are fitted with a side spike. When so fitted they are a very sound proposition.

Another question arises out of the subject of hooks. Should they be eyed or uneyed?

The eyed hook is a definite necessity on some of the tackles described, but except in these cases we are inclined to favour the uneyed. The advantages of the eyed treble are its simplicity of attachment and the security thereof. The security of the eye attachment is obviously greater that that of a whipping, and for this reason it is the usual thing to use eyed hooks when in search of big game fish. Against this however there is no denying the extra bulk caused by the eye. On paper this may sound a bit exaggerated but the angler who has any doubts should compare eyed and uneyed trebles of the same size. The difference is surprising.

Thus we recommend the eyed treble for use only on those tackles which are of a pattern actually requiring this type. For all other styles, and particularly on the smaller editions, we recommend the uneyed hook.

*   *   *   *   *

One of the greatest problems of the designer of spinning gear is the making of an unobtrusive tackle which will nevertheless hold the bait securely. The problem has never been satisfactorily solved, but there are one or two modifications which make for improvement.

The first is a side spear—a short length of sharpened wire which runs at right angles to the gut and is driven

into the fleshiest part of the bait. If the flesh is firm
the spear should give reasonable security, especially if it
is used in conjunction with a body spear and body hooks.

A piece of rustless steel wire of one inch or slightly longer
is bent into a right-angle as illustrated and the short side

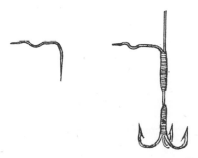

FIG. 30.   THIS SIDE SPEAR GIVES GREATER SECURITY

is whipped to the hook-length of gut or wire, or, if desired,
to the hook shank itself. (Fig. 30.)

Another aid to security concerns the spear. This,
instead of being wire, can be made of a narrow strip of
thin metal—brass, copper, or zinc—thus having a greater
hold inside the body of the bait. It is particularly useful
when spinning with deep-bodied fish like roach. These
offer a big resistance to spinning and are apt to twist over
on a wire spear.

The metal used should be very thin. Cut into the
illustrated shape and insert a propeller, of the pattern
shown, in the bend at the head. If desired the vane, in
addition to the spear, can be cut from metal, in which
case the two are soldered together. If, on the other hand,
celluloid is used, the strip metal of the spear should be
doubled back over the vane and secured with a binding.
This style is shown in the sketch. After securing the vane,
a hole is drilled in the position shown; pass a split ring
through the hole, and attach a swivel and hook flight.
(Fig. 31.)

If so desired the spear can be barbed with a file as shown
in C, or left plain as in A and B.

E

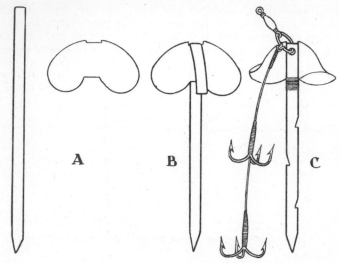

FIG. 31.   A REVOLVING TACKLE WITH FLAT SPEAR, VERY SUITABLE
FOR DEEP-BODIED BAITS

On the patterns used for larger fish a stiff piece of wire can be bent into the shape shown in Fig. 32A. Actually the small loop at the top end should be made inside the eye of a swivel or split ring, but this is omitted so that the

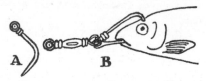

FIG. 32.   HEAD HOOK PREVENTS BAIT FROM SLIPPING DOWN THE
TACKLE ·

shape can be clearly shown. The following sketch shows how the spike is used ; here again the hook flight has been omitted for the sake of clearness. The point is driven into the head of the bait, thus preventing him from slipping down the spear.

All these extras will do their share in securing the bait to the tackle, but nevertheless a spool of thin wire or silk

in the pocket will often be worth its weight in gold.   A
few turns will give almost invisible security.

*   *   *   *   *

Fig. 33 shows four ways by which a hook flight may be
attached to a swivel, either directly or by means of a split
ring.   Other methods are shown in the chapter on knot-

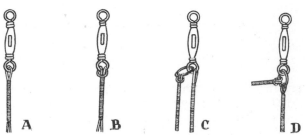

FIG. 33.   FOUR WAYS OF ATTACHING HOOK-FLIGHT TO
SWIVEL

tying.   The first method shown is only employed when the
gut is doubled throughout its length.   B and C are practically
the same as each other, the only difference being that the
latter is attached to a split ring instead of direct to the
swivel.

Method D is very useful if the eye of the swivel is over-
loaded.   Occasionally the number of attachments at the
head of the bait is more than the eye of the swivel can
comfortably accommodate.   When this occurs a small
split-ring should be threaded into the eye.   All other
attachments can then depend from the split-ring, instead
of from the eye direct.   This principle is practised in the
tackle shown in Fig. 19.

*   *   *   *   *

Fig. 34 shows two methods of bending a body spear
in order to obtain greater security.   The first is on the
same principle as a lady's hairpin ;   the bends help to hold
the wire inside the body of the bait.   The other consists
of a length of wire the end of which is doubled hard back as

shown, and a short length bent out to make a barb. The point can be slightly filed to assist penetration, but not to such an extent as to weaken the wire.

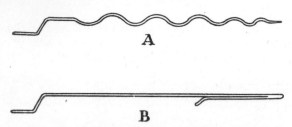

FIG. 34.   ALTERNATIVE TYPES OF BODY SPEAR

When making spinning tackles it should be borne in mind that the weakest spots are usually the knots, bindings, and other attachments. These points should therefore receive the most careful attention. The silk must always be well waxed to increase its holding power. The binding should be made as tightly as possible and should be generously varnished when completed. Points of friction, such as where a length of gut or wire passes through the eye of a swivel or hook, should be made as strong as possible. When the style of attachment will allow it is a good plan to pass the wire or gut twice through the eye before binding   The extra turn will do much to reduce the possibilities of a break.

III

ARTIFICIAL LURES

HERE is a subject which would fill volumes if dealt with fully. Fortunately this is unnecessary as the main types fall into a few standard groups. Once the general principles of each group are grasped the angler can make many varieties of each type. The knowledge gained thereby may be an incentive to him to use his powers of invention in evolving new patterns. That there is always a ready sale for something new and good in fishing tackle, is amply proved by the popularity of plug baits, thread-line reels, and multipliers, to name but three items of angling equipment which have achieved great success in recent years. Thus may an inventive angler derive substantial profit from his efforts.

Plug Baits.

The plug bait is so much in demand at present that we will give it first place in our list of artificial lures. It can be used in all sizes from ¾ of an inch upwards, which makes it suitable for trout, perch, pike, sea-trout, salmon and bass. Recent experiments have indicated that this lure will take fish when all others have failed. Add to this the fact that it is an extremely pleasant and fascinating tackle to use, and it is small wonder that the angling fraternity has received it with open arms.

The larger plug baits vary in price from 2s. 6d. to 6s. 6d., according to pattern and finish. This is rather an expensive item, and it is a blow indeed if the lure is lost while fishing.

Although it is well-nigh impossible for the amateur to reproduce the beautiful finish of the shop-bought product, it is nevertheless easy for him to copy its shape. This gives the action, which is quite as important as the finish.

We doubt if the fish are fastidious as to the latter, providing that the colours are attractive.

In making plug baits for our own use we have found that it does not pay to carve the body portion by hand as is recommended by some writers. A wood-turner will turn out a dozen blanks of various sizes for two shillings, and the result is much truer than the angler could hope to make by hand carving.

The dimensions will have to be decided by due consideration of the type of fish to be fished for. Trout and perch sizes need not exceed $1\frac{1}{4}$ inches in length, and sea-trout sizes should be only slightly longer. Pike, salmon, and bass patterns vary in length from two to six inches though the very long ones are used only under special circumstances. A good average size for these larger fish is three inches.

The thickness of the body varies according to the length. The following table gives a few suggested dimensions. The figures are approximate and can be varied slightly to suit the pattern in hand.

$\frac{3}{4}$	inch long—	$\frac{5}{16}$	inch thick.		
1	,,	,,	—$\frac{3}{8}$	,,	,,
$1\frac{1}{2}$	,,	,,	—$\frac{7}{16}$	,,	,,
2	,,	,,	—$\frac{5}{8}$	,,	,,
3	,,	,,	—$\frac{3}{4}$	,,	,,

The largest patterns should not exceed $\frac{7}{8}$ inch thickness.

Having decided which of the above sizes is most suitable for your fishing, go to the wood-turner and ask him to make the size required in one or other of the shapes shown in Fig. 35. Shape A is suitable for small single hook plugs; shape B is for larger sizes, carrying two or three trebles; shape C is a tapering body which is rapidly increasing in the angler's favour though it is more suitable for plugs incorporating a metal vane than for those on which the vane is carved into the head. When placing your order insist on a good smooth finish. Cedar and beech are the best woods.

*   *   *   *   *

We will start with a small trout pattern.

The first job is to make the sloping vane at the head of the plug. On this the diving action depends. A small gouge is used to carve the head into the scoop shape shown

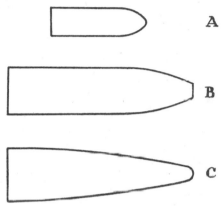

FIG. 35. BLANKS FOR PLUG-MAKING
(The section is round.)

in Fig. 36A. The mean angle of the slope varies between 35 and 45 degrees. It is vital that the shape be absolutely balanced on either side. Any slight inequality will put the plug out of commission, or at least will produce an undesirable action.

Bore a hole in the vane running downwards at an angle, so that its other end is a little less than midway along the belly of the plug (Fig. 36B). Drill another hole about a $\frac{1}{4}$ inch behind the first as shown by the dotted lines in the same sketch. Starting from the top side $\frac{1}{8}$ inch behind the last hole drill another about $\frac{1}{4}$ inch deep. This also is shown by a dotted line. These holes should be made with a drill of $\frac{1}{32}$ inch or $\frac{3}{64}$ inch diameter. The first hole should be countersunk to a depth of $\frac{1}{8}$ inch with a drill of $\frac{7}{64}$ inch diameter.

Take three inches of brass wire (gauge 22 or 23) and form a very small loop at one end as described in the chapter on wirework. Pass the free end into the hole at the head of the plug and bring it out below the belly. Thread a treble (size 8 to 6) on to the wire and push the wire up through the second hole. The round-jawed pliers mentioned in " Wirework " are very suitable for manœuvring the wire into position.

We now have the loop and the treble in their permanent positions but the spare wire is sticking up from the back of

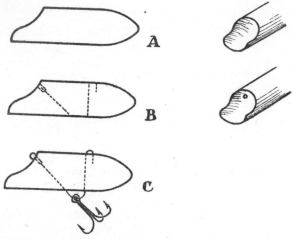

FIG. 36.   SINGLE HOOK PLUGS
A = Head scooped out.   B = Holes drilled.   C = Wire and treble fitted.

the bait. Cut all this away except about $\frac{5}{16}$ inch. This should be doubled into the small hole just behind. A diagram of a section of the plug showing the wire in position, is given in Fig. 36c.

If the bend of wire on the top of the back shows an inclination to stick out beyond the contour of the plug, this can be tapped home with a light hammer. The fitting described is perhaps a little tedious but it has the advantage of being very secure.

The next job is painting, and for this we recommend the sixpenny tins of synthetic paint described as lacquer. They are sold in a wide variety of colours and give a very good finish. Before applying the paint, however, it is necessary to give the wood a good coat of knotting. Then apply a coat of white paint, which makes an excellent background for any subsequent colour scheme.

The finished colour is a matter for the angler's taste. A useful effect can be obtained by shading down from olive green on the back, to silver on the sides, and white on the belly.

* * * * *

An alternative hook-mounting arrangement, suitable for small single treble plugs, can be made by binding a suitably-sized uneyed treble to a short length of stout gut. A small round bead is threaded on to the gut and brought down to the shank of the hook. This is intended to act as a stop. The free end of the gut is passed through a hole drilled from head to belly (Fig. 37).

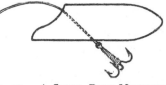

FIG. 37. A SMALL PLUG MOUNTED ON GUT

Some anglers prefer a single Limerick hook on trout-size plugs. This can be mounted by drilling the usual hole from the head downwards, and mounting an eyed-hook (size 4, 5, or 6) on to a length of fine rustless trace-wire. An eye is made in one end of the wire, the hook is threaded on, and the short end of wire is then twisted round its main length. (See " Wirework ").

Pass the free end of the wire through the hole in the plug bringing it out at the head. Form a similar eye close up against the head and cut away the surplus wire (Fig. 38).

The use of screw eyes, as described later, is not recommended on the smaller lures.

FIG. 38. SMALL PLUG WITH LIMERICK HOOK

* * * *

The home-made plug is a rather uncertain quantity. By this we do not mean it is unreliable, but rather that each requires a certain amount of individual treatment before it is perfect in action. The reason is obvious, for being hand-made they are each subject to slight variations which tend to make them erratic in the execution of their work. Thus, out of a batch of a dozen plugs we may get one or two that do not dive satisfactorily. Others tend to roll over, while some show a decided inclination to take a permanent right or left turn while being fished back to the angler.

These eccentricities are due to the slight inequalities which are inevitable in a hand-made article. In machine-made tackles, which can be shaped with mathematical precision, faults are reduced to a minimum.

The said variations can be corrected, however, by observing a few simple rules. For instance if the plug does not dive correctly, or if it displays a tendency to roll over, this can be remedied by adding a little weight to act as a keel. Drill a small hole as low down as possible in the head of the lure in the position indicated in Fig. 39. Into this

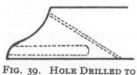

FIG. 39. HOLE DRILLED TO RECEIVE LEAD SHOT

insert one or two shot (according to the size of the plug) and stop up the hole with putty. The result is twofold ; the head is given a downward inclination which will assist diving, and the low position of the lead will prevent any tendency to roll.

If the lure tends to swerve to one side or the other in the water the fault lies in one of three positions. The wire eye in the head may not be dead-central, thus resulting in an uneven pull ; the hook mount may not be absolutely in the bottom centre of the belly, which causes an uneven keel ; or the gouging of the head may be slightly unequal which would result in one side offering a greater water resistance than the other, thus causing "swerve." The cure in each case is obvious.

*   *   *   *   *

In two-hook plugs the only material difference lies in the mounting of the trebles. The head is gouged in the same way, but this time we must drill holes as illustrated in Fig. 40A. These are drilled from head and tail respectively and they end on the lower side of the body at a distance of half an inch apart. At the head and tail each is slightly countersunk to accommodate the finishing turns of the wire eye.

Take a piece of brass or rustless steel wire (gauge 20 or 21) and form a small eye at one end. Pass the other end into the head and bring out at the belly. Thread on an

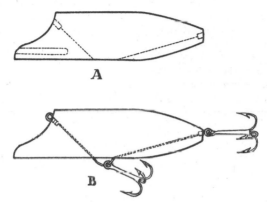

FIG. 40. DRILLING AND HOOK MOUNTING OF LARGER PLUGS

eyed treble (from No. 4 to No. 1 according to the size of the plug in hand) ; then pass the free end of wire through the other hole and bring it out at the tail. Pull the wire as tight as possible so that the head eye is in position and the treble is held tight against the body. Bend an eye close up to the tail end and mount the tail treble.

Even though the angler takes every precaution to keep the wire tight, a little slackness will have occurred by the time the last treble is mounted. This can be turned to good account by pulling down the wire which holds the body treble. This will pull the head and tail eyes tightly into position and will form a loop for the body treble to work in (Fig. 40B).

*   *   *   *   *

A quick and simple mount can be effected by the use of screw eyes. Some anglers swear by their efficiency but there can be no doubt that they are not so secure as the method just described. In experiments with these we have found that a fairly strong screw eye, well mounted, will not readily pull out of close-grained wood, but we suspect that there is a possibility of the eye opening, thus freeing the hook. A more improbable danger is that of the eye becoming unscrewed by a revolving fish. Their chief recommendation is their simplicity.

Brass screw eyes as sold by ironmongers are a trifle too large in the eye in the strength required for hook mounting. Strength, plus a good length of screw thread, are the main necessities. The eye itself can be reduced to any desired size by opening it up, cutting away the surplus, and re-uniting in its smaller form.

When inserting into the wood do not screw them in the same line as the ultimate fishing strains. If the shank of the screw eye is at a slight angle to the line of pull, the

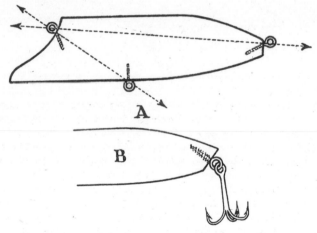

FIG. 41.   SCREW EYES FOR HOOK MOUNTING

See that these are screwed in at an angle to the fishing strains (the dotted lines).

B.   AN ALTERNATIVE MOUNTING FOR THE TAIL TREBLE

possibility of pulling out will be reduced to a minimum. Fig. 41 will make this clear. The lines of pull are indicated by the dotted lines, and the shanks of the screw eyes are set at an angle thereto.

With regard to the tail treble it is a good plan to adopt the style of mounting shown in Fig. 41B. The end of the plug is trimmed off with an upward slope as shown, and any rough edges left by the saw are smoothed down with sandpaper. A screw eye inserted at the appropriate angle will be much more secure than one which is screwed in, in the ordinary way. It is always a good idea to slightly countersink the wood at the positions where the screw eyes are to be inserted; this allows the eye to enter a little further into the wood and results in a much neater finish. An eye which projects too far is very unsightly.

*   *   *   *   *

Most of the larger sizes of plugs, due to their extra buoyancy, require a few shot in the head to give them a satisfactory diving action. The method has been previously described, but the number must be increased to suit the size of the lure. A large size will carry as many as five big shot. To get some idea of the number required the plug can be tested for buoyancy in a bowl of water.

*   *   *   *   *

Before passing on to the subject of jointed plugs, perhaps mention should be made of a few alternative patterns of head vanes. These have purposely been left until the present stage in order to save the reader from confusion.

The type so far mentioned is simple—just a scoop formed at the head—but it is more satisfactory in the smaller sizes than in the larger. For the latter many other designs can be tried to advantage, some of them embodying a metal or celluloid vane to augment their action.

A very effective shape, for which we believe we can justly claim originality, is a slight variation of that already described.

At a point one quarter of the distance from the head to the tail cut two flat surfaces at an angle to each other so that they give a pent-shaped appearance to the head. A chisel is the best tool for the job but it must be used with discretion, as the two surfaces must be true and absolutely equal in area and shape. As will be seen in Fig. 42, the surfaces not only slope away from each other but they also

slope downwards towards the head, at which point the
plug is reduced to almost half its normal depth.

When these surfaces are satisfactorily shaped the scoop

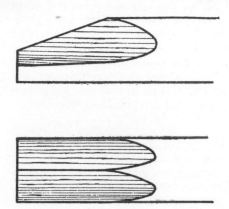

FIG. 42. ANOTHER TYPE OF HEAD (FIRST STAGE)

is added by cutting away the lower half of the head with a
gouge, taking great care that the ridge between the two
surfaces forms a central line to the head of the scoop.

Mounting is carried out as
before, the head attachment
being affixed at the point where
the ridge meets the scoop. All
this sounds very complicated
when verbally expressed but it
is simplified by a study of Figs.
42 and 43.

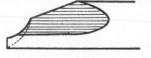

In our opinion the action of
this pattern, when properly
balanced and weighted, leaves
nothing to be desired. It dives
nicely, swims attractively, and
will please both the angler and
the fish.

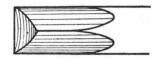

FIG. 43. SECOND STAGE OF
FIG. 42

*   *   *   *   *

Fig. 44 illustrates a head incorporating a metal vane.

This has the advantage of also acting as a keel in preventing the lure from rolling over. To accommodate the vane, cut into the plug at the head at an angle of about 45 degrees. (Fig. 44A.) An accurate cut can be made with a small tennon saw. Now make a second cut as illustrated so that a wedge-shaped piece of wood is completely removed from the head. Cut a piece of thin sheet zinc into the shape of B and drill two small holes to admit the screws which hold the plate in position. Fold over on the dotted line to the same angle as the cut-away in the head. Secure with two small round-head brass screws and trim

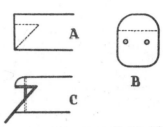

FIG. 44.   HEAD INCORPORATING METAL VANE

away any overlapping edges except those at the bottom of the vane.

The previously described methods of cast attachment cannot be easily applied to this pattern owing to its peculiar shape. A better way is to drill a hole downwards from the top of the head as indicated in Fig. 44c, care being taken to make this absolutely central. A thin brass screw or nail is driven into the hole and the hook-swivel of the cast is attached to that part which runs vertically between the "jaws" of the plug. The trebles are attached by means of screw eyes.

FIG. 45.   OTHER PATTERNS OF METAL VANE

Some of the difficulties attending this pattern can be obviated by using the type illustrated in Fig. 45A. Saw off the head of the plug at the appropriate angle and attach a perfectly plain metal vane. An improvement can be made by slightly curling the edges of the metal to give it a scoop effect. Hook and cast attachment can be made according to taste. Fig. 45B shows another type of metal vane. The metal is bent at an angle and screwed to a flat surface on the underside of the head.

A design which gives a fascinating action can be evolved by combining the ridge-backed pattern (Fig. 43) with a metal vane. It is as well to remember that all these vanes work much more satisfactorily if made slightly scoop-shaped. These are infinitely superior to the flat type.

*   *   *   *   *

Hitherto we have described only rigid bodied plugs. The jointed variety have achieved great popularity, especially in the larger sizes. Their chief advantage is that they are much more life-like ; when in the water their movements are almost as sinuous as those of a live fish.

The diving action of a plug is achieved by a special shape which causes water resistance to overcome buoyancy. In similar fashion the jointed plug is so designed that after diving, the water currents set in motion by the head are played upon the tail in a manner that produces that " fetching " wobble.

Fig. 46 shows two views of a jointed plug. As will be

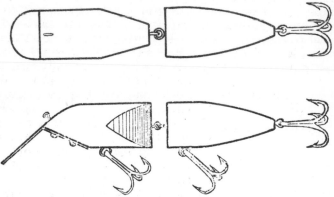

FIG. 46.   JOINTED PLUG—TOP AND SIDE VIEW
Note flattened surfaces at rear end of head

seen, the rear end of the head portion is shaved away to produce a flat, vertical surface on each side, whereas the front end of the tail piece is the full width of the plug.

When the plug is drawn towards the angler, the **water** planes off these converging surfaces alternately with the result that it hits up against the front end of the tail piece causing it to wobble from side to side.

There is no need to mention more than the chief differences between these and the rigid plugs. The head must be of the metal vaned type for the sake of its extra power. The angle of the flat surfaces to each other varies slightly according to individual requirements. A little experimenting will soon suggest the correct setting. The two halves are joined by screw eyes linked one within the other. These must be screwed absolutely in the centre of each end. Three trebles are more popular than two. Attach them as shown, also by means of screw eyes.

* * * * *

Before leaving this subject a few words about colour schemes may be useful. It is impossible to generalize on the matter owing to the variation in conditions under which the plug is used and the different fish which it is intended to beguile. To imitate your quarry's natural prey is perhaps the safest thing of all, though it is indeed hard to produce, with mere paint, the beauty of a fish's colouring.

A white or silvery belly is almost standardized and should be shaded up to olive green, steel blue, or brown. If the plug is intended to look like a roach a little dab of red can be added where the fins should be. The so-called pike finish is reputed second to none for pike spinning, and though the angler may not be able to achieve the professional finish he can nevertheless produce a goodly likeness by using green, yellow, silver and white in suitable proportions.

Shading is not always easy but can be greatly simplified by the use of gold paint powder and silver powder, which can be bought from any paint shop. Paint the back of the plug green and the belly white, then blow a little powder along the body where the two colours meet. The powder will stick to the wet paint and will completely obliterate the dividing line between the two colours. The result will be a white underside shading up through silver, to a green back—an attractive and natural effect. The

F

same scheme can be used with many other combinations of colours.

Occasionally a plug of extra visibility is required to overcome bad conditions of light and water. When this occurs the type illustrated in Fig. 47 is recommended. Along the body on each side are a series of vertical gouge cuts. These are smoothed with fine sandpaper and painted

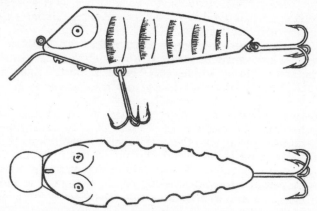

FIG. 47.   PLUG WITH " FACET " BODY, FOR INCREASED VISIBILITY
IN BAD CONDITIONS OF LIGHT

(*With acknowledgments to Mr. H. E. Towner Coston.*)

a bright colour. Better still, cut some oval pieces of silver paper and glue them into position in the grooves. To enhance visibility the body also can be covered with silver paper if desired, and painted a normal colour on the back. The whole lot is then varnished as a protection against water.

These grooves in the sides of the plug act in the same way as the facets of a diamond ; they catch and reflect the light from various angles. Their glint will catch the eye of a fish when other lures are invisible.

Spoons and Metal Lures

A few designs of metal lures can be made at home. These are simple types requiring no expensive tools or machinery. Others, such as Devon minnows, etc., are beyond the scope of the amateur tackleist in view of the special equipment used in their manufacture. We have yet to see a satisfactory home-made Devon excepting those made by anglers who are fortunate enough to possess a lathe.

Spoons can be cut from a copper cistern ball. Almost any size can be made in most of the leading shapes. Figs. 48 and 49 give some idea of various types of plain and bar

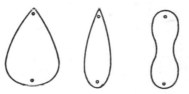

FIG. 48. THREE SHAPES OF PLAIN SPOONS

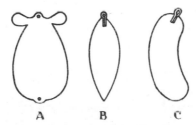

A   B   C

FIG. 49. THREE TYPES OF BAR SPOONS

spoons. The mounting for the former is very simple. A hole is drilled in the head and tail ends as illustrated, and a suitably sized treble is fitted by means of a split ring. A hook swivel is then fitted to the top hole.

As their name implies, the bar spoons rotate on a wire bar. At one end of this the cast is attached, while the other carries the treble.

The first of those illustrated is the Colorado, which is fitted with vanes at the head to assist propulsion. These arc cut in one piece with the rest of the spoon and can afterwards be twisted into a propeller shape. The spoon is fitted on to a wire bar (gauge 18 or 16), bent into the shape shown in Fig. 50, A or B. To make this, first bend

the lower loop on to the wire and thread a round glass bead
into the position shown. This will assist the rotation of
the lure. Pass the free end of wire through the spoon

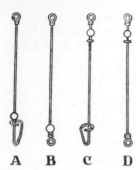

A   B   C   D

FIG. 50. BARS FOR BAR
SPOONS

bringing it out at the head, where
another loop (for cast attachment)
should be made. If type A loop
is used the hook can be attached
or changed at any time, but with
type B it must be threaded on
before the loop is closed.

*   *   *   *

The bar and kidney spoons differ
in their attachment from that of
the Colorado. They are attached
only at one end—the head—and
consequently the bead on which
they rotate is secured in a forward
position on the bar. The same

gauge of wire is used and is bent into the same shape, not
forgetting to leave the head loop until after the spoon is
fixed in position.

About ¾ of an inch below the ultimate position of the

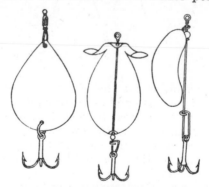

FIG. 51. THREE STYLES OF MOUNTING—PLAIN, COLORADO AND
KIDNEY

top loop, solder a ring of thin wire around the main bar.
This acts as a stop for the bead which is threaded on above
it. (Figs. 50 and 51.) Solder a wire eye to one end of the

spoon (Fig. 49, B and C) and bend this slightly inwards so that the spoon will lie snugly against the bar.   Pass this eye on to the bar above the bead and form a final loop at the head of the bar for attachment to the trace.   Fig. 51 shows the three main types mounted ready for use.

If a little extra weight is desired this can be added, in the form of lead wire, to the bar.   The plain (unbarred) spoons have no place to accommodate lead, but it can be fitted to the cast in the form of a fold-over lead.

*   *   *   *   *

Hook sizes depend entirely on the size of the spoon.   If they are too small the spoon itself will form a barrier to penetration, if too large they will tend to hinder the action. It is better, however, in the case of spoons, to err slightly on the large side.   For pike fishing trebles are sometimes decorated with red wool and tinsel — colours which are reputed to whet the pike's gory appetite.   Their value, even if used discriminately, is doubtful ; but to use them to the extent seen in tackle shops is positively detrimental. Not only are the trebles adorned with red tassels, but it is quite a common sight to see one entire side of a spoon painted the same colour.   Actually we could afford to dispense with this colour on pike lures, but if we do use it it should be applied very sparingly.   The effect should be reminiscent of the fins of a roach ; and not, as the tackle makers seem to think, of a Royal Mail van.

While on the subject of colour schemes we are reminded to point out that the copper cistern-ball, from which our spoons are cut, limits us to one shade.   Incidentally, bright copper is one of the finest colours for pike fishing. For the angler who likes variety, however, we would like to record that we have successfully used spoons made from dessert and table-spoons purchased at Woolworth's. The handles are removed and the hooks mounted in the usual way.

Spoons can also be made from flat sheet metal such as brass.   The thickness varies according to the size and weight of lure required.   The shape is cut out of the flat metal ; it is then layed on a wooden bench and tapped with a round-headed hammer.   It will soon curve into the required shape.   This method is worth consideration and study, for it enables the angler to produce spoons of very varied action. It is on the shape of the spoon, and the degree of scoop, that the action depends. A little experiment will produce fast spinners, slow spinners, wobblers, etc., all of which will attract fish. If desired the spoons can be plated, nickel or chromium, and colour added to taste.

*   *   *   *   *

Of late there has developed a considerable interest in the fishing of the Baited Spoon for flounders. The best spoon for the purpose is approximately the same shape as a table-spoon though slightly more pointed at the lip end. It is most essential that it should spin steadily even at very slow speeds. It is also essential that the bait which is carried on the hook should not revolve with the spoon. To this end a special hook attachment is necessary as shown in Fig. 52. A split-ring is passed through the top eye of the spoon and to this are attached a swivel for cast attachment and a chain of swivels for carrying the hook. Thus the spoon can revolve without in any way interfering with the baited hook.

FIG. 52.   METHOD OF MOUNTING HOOK FOR FISHING THE "BAITED SPOON" FOR FLOUNDERS

If a chain of swivels is unobtainable it can be made by uniting separate swivels with small split-rings until the chain is long enough to allow the hook to hang a couple of inches below the spoon. Hooks should be of the eyed O'Shaunessy type and of sizes varying between four and one. The smaller sizes are preferable. The hook is baited with lugworm, king ragworm, mussel or fish.

A glance at Fig. 52 will make any further explanation unnecessary.

    *   *   *   *   *

A sea spinner is shown in Fig. 53. This is cut from thin sheet metal, such as brass or copper, into the shape shown. The ends are first drilled and then turned over at right-angles. A brass wire bar, similar to those used for bar

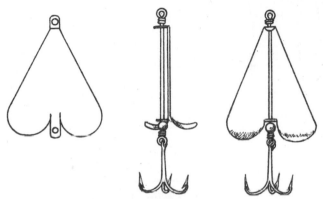

FIG. 53.   MACKEREL SPINNER

spoons (Fig. 50, A or B), is passed through the holes. A treble hook is attached to one end of the wire and the other is looped to receive the swivel ; the vanes are then bent into the propeller shape. This is quite a good lure for mackerel, pollack, and bass.

A variation, shown in the following illustration, consists of an elongated fish-shaped body, headed by the propeller fins. The lot is cut out in one piece of metal and can either be mounted as shown, or, alternatively, on a bar like that in the previous pattern.

An immense variety of spinning lures, suitable both for river and sea, can be made on the same lines as Fig. 54. Slight variations of colour, shape, and proportions, will have to be made to fit them for individual requirements.

Other Lures

The wagtail is a bait which has accounted for many

large fish. It is made of two pieces of rubber, a swivel, two or three trebles, some thin wire, some gimp, and a celluloid or metal propeller.

A piece of old motor inner tube is quite suitable for the

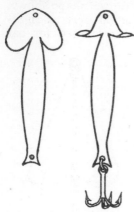

FIG. 54.   BASS OR POLLACK
SPINNER

rubber body, the shape of which is shown in the illustration (Fig. 55). The two halves are exactly the same shape but are placed " back to back " so that the tails point in opposite directions. The success of the wagtail is attributed to this feature, which is said to produce attractive vibrations in the water.

The peculiar shape of the propeller is calculated to give the greatest security to the body when it is finally attached. Before this can be done, however, a piece of gauge 20 or 21 brass or rustless steel wire is attached to the propeller and swivel. When making the final twists below the former a short length should be bent at right angles in the manner shown, the idea being to prevent the rubber body from twisting round on the body wire.

Bind the " nose " at the head of the rubber body to the projecting part of the propeller. Strong thread wrapped tightly will give a secure fit. Using a needle and thread, stitch the two pieces of rubber together at the point where the end of the wire runs at right angles to the main body wire. The tail ends of rubber should be left free.

All is now ready for the hooks to be fixed. The one at the tail lies in a loop made at the end of the wire. One or two more (according to choice) can be attached by means of wire to the lower eye of the head swivel. The underside of the bait is painted silver or gold ; and the back, green, brown or blue. Weight can be added by coiling lead wire around the body wire, though most anglers prefer to fish the wagtail with the lead on the cast, in which case the anti-kink type should be used. The completed

tackle is shown in Fig. 55 and can be made in a variety of
sizes from two to five inches.

*   *   *   *   *

In sea fishing the rubber worm, both red and black, is
extremely popular.   On some parts of the coast it is a
deadly bait for pollack and bass when trolled behind a
moving boat.   A piece of thin rubber gas tubing about
7 inches long forms the body, and is cut to a taper 3 inches

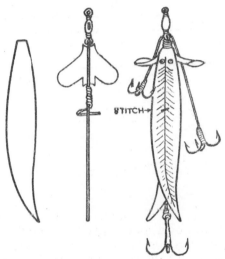

FIG. 55.   MAKING A WAGTAIL

from the tail end (Fig. 56A).   Bend a piece of stiff wire
(gauge 18) to the shape shown, and enclose a swivel in the
top eye and a large treble at the bottom.   Below the top
eye the finishing turns of wire should run down the body
wire for at least an inch to provide a non-slip surface on
which to secure the tubing (Fig. 56B).   The distance
between the eyes should be 4¼ inches.   The wire must be
bent into a decided curve to ensure good spinning properties.

Thread the wire into the tube and secure at the head
with a whipping of strong thread which should be varnished

for preservation. An extra hook can be fitted if desired by attaching a length of gut or trace wire to the top eye.

*   *   *   *   *

Sea fly-fishing is not very popular but is quite good sport in certain localities. The flies used are not always made of silk and feather; soleskin also has its adherents. It has the additional advantage of being suitable for very light trolling for mackerel and other surface fish.

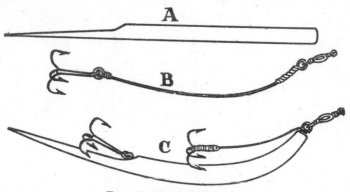

FIG. 56. RUBBER WORM

Any fishmonger will be only too pleased to give the angler a few skins from Dover soles. Lay these out flat on a board, remove all wrinkles and folds, and leave to dry in the sun. In a short time they will become as stiff as parchment.

A variety of shapes can be used, but those shown in Fig. 57 are the most popular. In A, a pear-shaped piece of skin is cut out and painted white or silver on the inside. On the outside the edges are painted silver shading up to blue or olive-green on the back. Thoroughly varnish both sides. If this is not done properly the water will get in and cause the skin to go limp.

Fold the fly down the centre, and whip it by the head to a suitably sized Limerick hook. The body part is thus allowed to move freely and gives an inviting action when fished by the sink-and-draw method.

The second shape is intended to represent a britt or

whitebait. It is treated in exactly the same way but is slightly longer and thinner in shape. An optional difference can be effected by stitching the two lower edges together

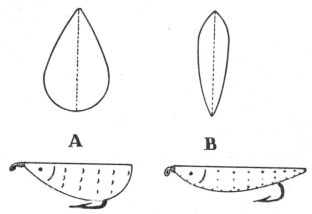

FIG. 57.   SOLESKIN LURES

to form a compact body in which, if desired, a little lead wire can be added round the shank of the hook.

Quite a passable representation of a sand-eel can be made from soleskin by cutting into the shape illustrated in Fig. 58A. Use two or three hooks according to length and

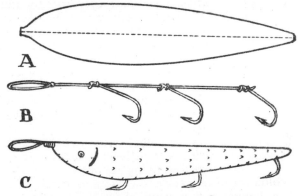

FIG. 58.   SANDEEL MADE WITH SOLESKIN

secure these to strong gut substitute or rustless trace wire. Eyed hooks are best as they give extra security. Thread the hooks on to the wire or gut and secure at suitable intervals. Add lead wire if necessary ; fold the prepared soleskin over the flight and secure at the head with a binding of thread. Stitch the two lower edges together, and colour as usual.

The body of the finished lure is rather thin. If a plumper body is required a little packing should be inserted before stitching the edges together.

The sand-eel is a grand bait for bass and pollack, but unfortunately it is not always obtainable. An artificial such as this will often yield good sport when trolled behind a boat. A good silvery finish is essential in order that the lure shall imitate the natural fish as nearly as possible. To this end silver paint can be used, but a better effect can be obtained by glueing a sheet of silver paper over the body and varnishing over.

* * * * *

Another useful sand-eel lure can be made from a length of rubber tubing six inches in length and a quarter of an inch in diameter. White rubber is preferable to any other colour, but if this is not obtainable red will do. It is cut as shown in Fig. 59A ; the V-shape at the top end represents the mouth, and the taper at the lower end represents the tail.

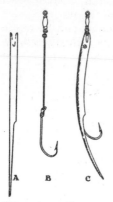

Other requirements include a short length of stiff wire, gauge 18 ; an eyed hook size 2/0 or 3/0 ; and a swivel. Attach the hook and swivel to the wire as shown in Fig. 59B ; the overall length should be about four inches. Pass this along the tube so that the " jaws " of the sand-eel are just below the lower end of the swivel. In this position they

FIG. 59. SANDEEL MADE WITH RUBBER TUBE

can be bound with waxed thread. The wire is then bent in a curve to ensure a good spinning action.

The colouring of the tackle is a matter of taste. Personally we have found that a good effect can be obtained by painting the body silver, and the back a silvery green or blue ; the inside of the tail is also painted silver. An eye is added to increase the life-like effect, after which a generous coat of varnish completes the tackle.

By including a celluloid propeller the sand-eel can be made to revolve. This is shown in Fig. 60, and in view of previous instructions no further details are necessary. The

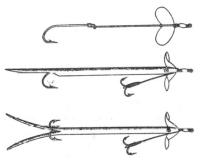

FIG. 60. REVOLVING SANDEEL, SUITABLE FOR SALT OR FRESH WATER

jaws, as will be seen, are made to overlap the propeller and are bound in at the head. If desired an extra hook can be attached as shown.

Another variation is seen in the following sketch. Instead of the tail being shaved down to a taper it is divided into two ; and a treble is fitted in place of the single hook. In action this lure is very similar to the wagtail, and can be used for spinning in salt or fresh water.

* * * * *

A variety of floating lures of the beetle, spider, and grasshopper types can be made by the use of cork. Good cork, free from cracks and faults, is used to shape the bodies, a selection of which is shown in Fig. 61. A rough shape can be carved with a sharp knife or razor blade, after which the finishing touches can be made with fine sandpaper. The tail end of the body should be fairly large ; the extra cork is necessary to buoy up the lower end of the hook.

With a knife cut a thin slit along the underside of the body, into which lay a hook of appropriate size. A dab of celluloid varnish around the shank, and in the slit, will secure the cork and prevent it from slipping round on the hook.

Bind at the head and between the segments so that the bait is firmly secured. Legs are made from stiff gut substitute which is threaded through needle holes pierced in the body of the cork, and which project to the correct distance on each side. The legs of the spider are knotted to give the effect of a bend in the leg.

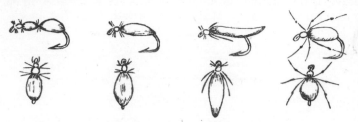

FIG. 61. TOP AND SIDE VIEW OF CORK LURES—BEETLES, GRASSHOPPERS, SPIDERS. ETC.

The artificial is now coloured as nearly as possible to the shade of its natural counterpart. Gold, silver, black, brown and green are all useful shades for the purpose.

Variations in colour schemes are obtained by making a few turns of peacock herl at the head or around the thorax, thus producing a metallic sheen which is very realistic.

When cast upon the water the hook acts as a keel and the bait always floats correctly.

*   *   *   *   *

The next section to be dealt with concerns feathered lures. Perhaps these really belong to the chapter on fly-tying, but as they do not resemble a fly in any other respect than the materials used, we prefer to classify them under the present heading, particularly as some of them incorporate a spinning vane at the head.

Peacock herl, claret hackles, whisks of red, and silver and gold tinsel are the most popular materials used in their construction. Patterns include grubs, caterpillars, shrimps, fry ; and fancy lures which do not bear any resemblance to living creatures but which rejoice in such names as " Devils," " Demons," Terriers " etc.

The principles by which these are constructed are very similar to those governing fly-tying. We propose therefore to deal with the main differences here, and suggest that the angler reads the chapter on fly-tying before making any of the lures mentioned.

To make the pattern illustrated in Fig. 62A three hooks of the desired size (11 to 6) are whipped to gut after the fashion of a Stewart tackle. Around the shank of each hook bind a length of gold or silver tinsel (see " Fly-tying "). Take a feather of slightly greater length than the tackle,

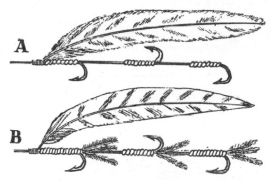

FIG. 62. FEATHERED LURES SUITABLE FOR TROUT AND SEA-TROUT

and of a bright or attractive colour, (white, black, red, badger or jungle cock are very suitable) and bind this in by the quill end to the head of the foremost hook, in such a manner that it forms a graceful curve over the flight. Varnish the binding with " Cellire."

Fig. 62B is the same tackle with the addition of tail whisks of peacock-herl. These must be secured with silk prior to the binding on of the tinsel.

Another pattern, made this time from a Pennell tackle, is shown in the next illustration (Fig. 63A). The materials are similar but the tinsel should be as thick as possible in order to make a substantial body, as this lure is intended to represent a small fish. Coil on as before but covering both hook-shanks and the intermediate length of gut. Silver is the best colour as this is the natural colour of the underside of a fish.

Select feathers with long fronds and bind two or three together at the head of the top hook. Run the fingers down to gather in any stray whisks and bind in again round the bottom hook. Snip away the quills protruding from the head whipping, and do not forget the varnish.

The colour scheme can be varied to suit the angler or the fish. Instead of the usual feathers down the back a bunch of peacock-herl can be used, tied as before at head and tail, and a hackle can be added if desired.

The " caterpillar " in Fig. 63B is made from peacock herl, gold ribbing, and red or cochy-bondhu hackles. For instructions for fixing these the angler is once again referred to the chapter on fly-tying. The body should be made fat and

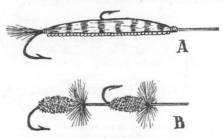

FIG. 63.   MORE FEATHERED LURES

round by generous use of the herl, and the ribbing must not be applied so tightly as to materially reduce the size thereof.

*   *   *   *   *

A popular pattern, which occasionally works wonders among the trout, bears a slight resemblance to the Alexandra fly and is shown in Fig. 64. Bind a treble hook (size 14 to 8) to a looped length of stiff gut substitute, leaving an eye at the head for cast attachment. The overall length varies between $\frac{3}{4}$ inch and 2 inches, the latter size being suitable for sea-trout etc. When securing the gut remember that the two ends should be bent round the bottom of the treble and returned a little way up the shank where they are bound in with the main length. This will prevent the ends from pulling out under fishing stresses (See " Hook Tackles ").

Form a body by wrapping silver tinsel or braid from the shank of the hook to the top eye (Fig. 64A) where a bunch of peacock herl is bound in so that it extends just beyond the treble. A few whisks of red bound in with the herl will add to the colour scheme.

At the throat add a bright coloured hackle—claret, red or blue are suitable—varnish the whipping and the lure should resemble Fig 64B.

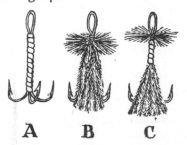

FIG. 64. LURE MADE FROM PEACOCK HERL—A POPULAR PATTERN

The other illustration is a slight variation using exactly the same materials. The herl is secured at the throat as before but the tinsel is wrapped *outside* it, thus forming a plump silver body, after which the hackle is added.

    *   *   *   *   *

The next sketch shows the making of a grub—not a very handsome grub, but one with which quite a few fish have been taken. It is made of wool and silver braid, the chief

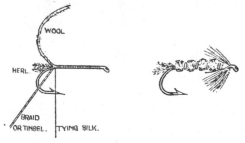

FIG. 65. MAKING A GRUB

difficulty being to obtain wool of the correct shade—a dirty grey olive. Failing all else a dirty white or cream colour will be found quite suitable.

G

The wool is wrapped round the shank of the hook in much the same way as when dressing a Palmer fly. This procedure is described in the chapter on fly dressing, and need not be repeated here. The only difference is that the grub requires a much fatter body, and this is obtained by a generous use of the wool. It may be necessary to wind on several thicknesses before the correct size is reached. The gold braid, which, as will be seen in " Fly Dressing," is tied in before the body is made, is then wound round in even coils from the tail to the head, and gives to the body a segmented effect.

Minor variations include a hackle at the head ; and a tuft of peacock herl, or a coloured tag, at the tail.

The lures described above are just a few of the great variety which can be concocted from fly-tying materials. Variations, such as size, colour, and shape can be made to suit the requirements of the moment. Weight can be added as desired by coiling lead wire around the hook shanks before the bodies are formed.

A major difference, a variation which transforms the lure into a revolving bait, is the addition of a spinning vane

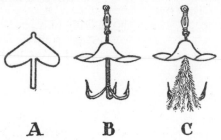

A   B   C

FIG. 66. AS FIG. 64, BUT FITTED WITH PROPELLER

at the head. The shape of the vane is shown in Fig. 66. The long thin body is securely bound to the shank of the head hook with strong thread, after which the work proceeds as before.

Obviously when using this propeller, a small swivel will be a necessary addition to the cast. The vanes of the propeller are bent to the desired angle by means of round-nosed pliers.

IV

FLY-DRESSING

THIS is one of the most absorbing studies in the craft of tackle-making. It embodies much more than the mere manipulation of fur and feather. A complete treatise would fill a capacious bookshelf and would include a knowledge of entomology, a study of the feeding habits and vision of fishes, and an observation of the effects of air, light, and water upon various materials.

The novice approaches the subject with mixed feelings. Though he may have the necessary enthusiasm to make him feel inclined to study it, he nevertheless thinks that it is something beyond his powers, something so involved and detailed as to prevent him from achieving success. This first paragraph will have done little to dispel such a point-of-view.

Such qualms however are quite unjustified and can be forgotten if he will content himself with " walking " before he essays to " run." Though fly-dressing is an involved subject it can be presented in easy stages which offer every encouragement to the beginner. This chapter must of necessity lack most of that fine detail which turns amateur work into fine craftsmanship, but it contains sufficient instruction to put the novice on the highroad to proficiency. We have no hesitation in saying that he will, within an hour of studying this chapter, be able to turn out a few flies suitable for immediate use, providing of course that the necessary materials are to hand. We will go further and say that unless the beginner is fastidious as to fine detail, he will learn sufficient from the following notes to enable him to do his own fly-tying for the rest of his angling career. The product of his labours may not equal in appearance those of the professional (which probably please the angler more than the fish) but it will nevertheless be business-like and effective.

If on the other hand the following " taste " whets the appetite for a " banquet " the reader is recommended to more detailed studies on the subject from the expert pens of Halford, West, Wooley, McClelland and other writers of note.

*   *   *   *   *

The other chapters in this work are intended to show the angler how to save money by the manufacture of his own tackle, besides presenting to him an interesting side-issue of his sport.

In fly-dressing the former quality is almost lacking but the latter is doubled. Very little financial saving can be effected by tying ones own flies. The tools are cheap enough and some of them are useful in other sections of tackle making ; but the materials, the feathers, furs, silks, tinsels etc., are by far the biggest item. If one could buy just the necessary amount of material for the number of flies to be tied, and at proportionate prices, there is no doubt that the saving would be great. Unfortunately however, we are obliged to purchase whole wings, necks, etc. in infinite variety for the various patterns. In course of time we find that we have accumulated a surplus to the value of several pounds.

Against this it is only fair to say that the angler who buys wisely can effect a slight saving, particularly if he is content with a modest selection—it is variety which costs money. And then, to come back to our original comparison, there is the deep and absorbing interest of the subject which provides ample recompense for the time and money spent thereon. Finally there is the advantage of a dressing which suits our requirements exactly, one which we ourselves have tied, and one for which we justly feel a glow of extra pride when a good fish is landed thereon.

The Equipment.

It is the usual thing to open up on the question of equipment with the advice that only the best (and most expensive) is good enough. We do not deny that the best tools will give the most satisfaction and the best results in the long run, but this point has been so unduly stressed in the past as to cause many a tyro to invest more than he could really afford, in the fond belief that it was impossible to do the work with cheaper equipment.

A fly-tyer's complete equipment comprises a special vice, two pairs of hackle pliers, a pair of scissors, one stilletto, and one pair of tweezers.

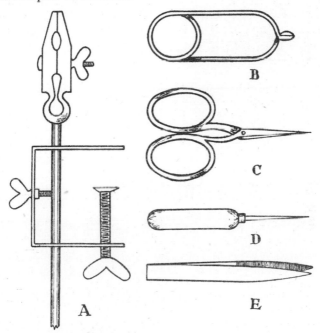

FIG. 67.   FLY-DRESSING TOOLS
A = Vice. B = Hackle Pliers. C = Scissors. D = Stiletto. E = Tweezers.

The vice may cost anything from 12/6 upwards.   If the angler cannot afford more he can purchase a very satisfactory pattern at this price.   Hackle pliers are cheap enough but should be bought with care.   See that they have a good spring action and that the surfaces of the jaws meet perfectly flat.   The latter point is very important.   It is as well to purchase one large and one small pair, as each has its uses at certain times. The stilletto and the tweezers offer no difficulties ; each can be bought for a few pence.

This leaves the scissors. They are the most important tools in the whole equipment and the only ones on which the angler is advised to " plunge " to the limit of his pocket. What is more, we advise that he does not trust his own discretion in their purchase but writes to a reliable tackle-maker who can be depended upon to forward the correct thing. Long, thin, close-cutting blades are absolutely essential, and these are not to be obtained in the cheaper grades.

Other indispensible items include wax, celluloid varnish, and shellac varnish.

*   *   *   *   *

As regards the flies themselves the first necessity is an adequate supply of Eyed Hooks in sizes from 6 to 14 (old scale). These should be small in the eye, fine in the wire, and needle sharp.

Tying Silks can be obtained in immense variety but a useful selection includes black, fiery brown, olive, blue dun, crimson, orange, and purple. These can be used in tying a great variety of flies, but other shades will be found necessary from time to time. Details of the precise colour for each fly are found by consulting the list of dressings.

Dyed Seal's Fur is one of the most popular materials for forming bodies. The best colours are those already mentioned for tying silks, but the lake angler may also require green and blue. Mole's and hare's furs are also very useful in their natural undyed state.

Floss Silks are also used for making bodies. Generally speaking they are only used in the brighter shades such as crimson, green, blue, etc., but as a body material they are inferior to seal's fur and are gradually falling out of favour.

Peacock Herl in bronze and green shades is a wonderful representation of the metallic sheen of such flies as the Coachman, Cochybondu, or Alder. For black bodies Black Ostrich Herl can be used.

Quills—i.e. stripped fronds of peacock herl—are obtainable in several shades, the most used being blue dun, olive, and natural. They are used when it is desired to give the body a segmented effect.

The only other body materials which the beginner is likely to require are gold and silver Tinsels. These form the ribbing, which may be either round, like wire, or flat. There are various widths and thicknesses.

Now for a few Hackles. A small opening stock should include Blue Dun, Cochybondu, Olive (various shades), Red and Black. A few brighter colours, such as crimson, green, blue and claret may be required by the angler who is tying flies for lake fishing. For dry flies the hackles should be from the cock bird ; bright, stiff, and full of life, not old, brittle, and faded. Hen hackles, which are much softer, are used on wet flies. The longer fibres, from the butt of the hackle, make excellent tail whisks.

Wings are rather an expensive item and we advise that in the early stages the stock be limited to Starling, Snipe and Woodcock ; with the addition of Grouse and the breasts of Mallard and Teal for the lake fisher. Wings must be bought in matched pairs.

To enumerate all the above requirements will no doubt give the reader the impression that the outlay for fly-dressing is very considerable, whereas actually a humble start can be made for an outlay of thirty or forty shillings.

Description of Types

Trout flies (which are also suitable for grayling, chub and other coarse fish) are divided into two main types— wet or dry. These are sub-divided again into winged flies and hackle (or wingless) flies. Brief descriptions are as follows :—

(1) The Winged Dry Fly is a floating fly often bearing a passable resemblance to a natural fly. Stiff cock's hackles keep it afloat and wings add to its lifelike appearance.

(2) The Hackle Dry Fly is similar in every respect except that it has no wings. These are more often used in the Northern waters whereas the winged variety find favour on the chalk-streams of the South.

(3) The Winged Wet Fly is a soft-hackled fly with the wing lying over the back—not cocked as is usual in the case of the dry fly. The body materials are such that

the fly sinks readily below the surface of the water. Most lake flies fall into this category.

(4) The Hackle Wet Fly is similar to the above but wingless. A great favourite in fast water.

Perhaps the foregoing is already well known to the reader, but we have segregated the types in this fashion as each differs from the other in methods of tying or in materials used.

We propose in the following pages to deal with each type in turn, but not in the same order as above. The simplest styles will be studied first in order to make the beginner's task as light as possible.

Hackle Dry Flies

One of the simplest flies imaginable, from the point of view of materials, colour, and dressing, is the Black Spider. It is obviously a suitable fly for a beginner's first effort.

Take one of the largest hooks and put it in the vice; the shank must be horizontal and pointing to your right. The vice grips the hook from the point to the bend, but

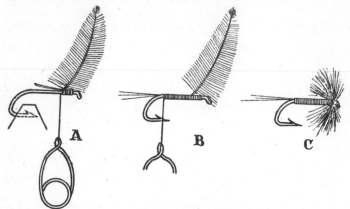

FIG. 68. MAKING A HACKLE DRY FLY
Two hackles can be used if desired.

the point must not be allowed to protrude from the jaws or it will interfere with the manipulation of the silk. The grip can be seen in Fig. 68A.

Take ten inches of black tying-silk and wax it well. Take also a black cock's hackle and remove the longer fibres from around the butt. Three of the longest of these are put on one side to use as whisks. Holding the tip of the hackle in a pair of hackle tweezers draw the finger and thumb down the feather so that the fibres stand out at right angles to the stem. Fig. 69 shows the removal of the surplus fibres and the general appearance of the remainder after they have been rubbed up. These are all the materials required and are now ready for use.

Starting about one-sixteenth of an inch away from the eye, wind the silk in close tight turns along the shank towards the tail. Stop when six turns have been laid on, and cut away

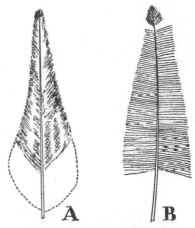

FIG. 69. PREPARING A HACKLE

A = Long fibres removed.
B = Remaining fibres brushed down.

the short end of silk around which the long end has been coiled. Pick up your feather in the left hand and lay its butt on to the hook-shank at the end of the binding (Fig. 68A). Wind the silk around shank and butt still working downwards to the tail. When the latter is reached cut off the protruding end of the butt.

Pick up the three tail whisks between the finger and thumb of the left hand. Hold them closely together and lay on the rear end of the hook shank. Start rewinding the silk around whisks and shank, this time working back towards the eye, which means, of course, that you will be laying another coil on top of your original body (Fig 68B). Continue winding this coil until you have passed the hackle and have arrived at your first turn of silk.

As the reader has but one pair of hands he may by now be wondering how all this picking up, winding, and cutting can be accomplished without letting go of the tying silk and thus allowing the windings to slacken. While the actual windings are in progress the fingers offer by far the most efficient grip and the most sensitive working touch. When it is necessary to let go the silk simply clip it between the hackle pliers, and leave these hanging from the hook at the end of the silk. Their weight will be quite sufficient to hold the coils in position (Fig. 68A). Alternatively some vices are equipped with a rubber screw-pad into which the silk can be fastened when desired.

We have now formed the body and tail of our fly. All that remains is to wind on the hackle and finish off.

Leaving the larger pair of hackle pliers hanging from the silk, take the small pair and grip the tip of the hackle. Start to wind the hackle slightly towards the head of the fly by making close turns around the shank, but keeping always behind the hanging end of the tying silk.

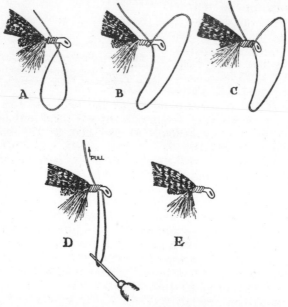

FIG. 70.   THE WHIP FINISH AT THE HEAD OF A FLY

Immediately your fly begins to look like the real thing. Stiff, glossy black fibres stick out in all directions in the approved manner. When you are satisfied that sufficient turns have been made, allow the pliers holding the hackle to hang down in the manner previously described. Throughout the process of manipulating the hackle the utmost care is necessary to avoid a break. The tip particularly, where the pliers grip, is a very weak point and will quickly snap if jerked or pulled too hard.

Pick up your tying silk again and bind the tip of the hackle to the shank of the hook. Three or four turns are sufficient after which the superfluous tip should be cut away with scissors.

Finally, in the sixteenth of an inch of naked shank left below the eye, form a whip finish of about four turns (Fig. 70). Varnish this with shellac and the fly is complete.

Assuredly nothing could be easier than this initiation into fly-dressing. If the reader had any qualms when embarking on his first attempt, we hope that these have now been dispelled, and that he is willing to attempt something a little more complicated but not necessarily more difficult.

*   *   *   *   *

The next example is a Blue Upright. It is not a big step forward, its only material difference being the addition of a quill body.

Place all the materials in readiness before starting. They consist of ten inches of waxed silk (the colour is immaterial so long as it does not contrast too noticeably with the slatey blue of the hackles), a strip of light peacock quill, a blue dun cock hackle, and three tail whisks of the same shade.

It is usual to tie this fly with a fairly long hackle—a point which should be remembered when this is selected.

Proceed exactly as before up to the point where the tail whisks are tied in, and secure these with two turns of silk. Before making the following turn, insert the end of the quill between the shank and the silk to secure it in the position shown in Fig. 71A, after which, forgetting the quill for the present, continue winding back again until the hackle is *almost* reached. Attach hackle pliers to the

silk and leave this " parked " while proceeding with the
winding of the quill.

Take the free end of the quill between the fingers and
commence winding in flat consecutive coils towards the
head. (Fig. 71B.) It will be seen that the quill so wound

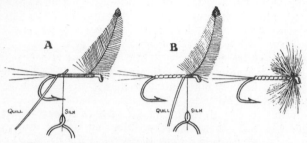

FIG. 71.   SHOWING HOW A QUILL BODY IS MADE

gives a remarkable resemblance to the segments of the
body of a natural fly. Continue winding until near the
hackle where the silk has been temporarily parked. When
this point is reached cease winding the quill, and bind it
in position with two turns and a half hitch of silk. Cut
away the surplus quill and continue winding the silk until
the head of the fly is reached. In passing the hackle take
care to avoid trapping any of the fibres under the turns of
silk.

It is now time to coil the hackle and fasten off in the
same manner as before, after which a touch of varnish
completes the fly.

This gives us two types of body, one of tying silk and
the other of quill. There are other styles which can be
applied to the hackle dry fly, but we propose to deal with
the more advanced stages of body-building under subsequent headings. The reader must remember that they
are to a certain extent interchangeable. The chief point
to bear in mind in this connection is that dry-fly bodies
should be constructed as far as possible from materials
which do not absorb water—for obvious reasons. In the
same way hackles should be stiff, glossy cock hackles
which hold the fly well up on the water. Soft hen hackles
and absorbent bodies are most suited to wet flies.

There are many other methods of achieving the results described above ; in fact each writer on the subject has something different to suggest. Some would prefer to make the body first, and tie in the hackle afterwards. Others suggest that the hackle be tied in by the point and not by the butt. Some would reinforce the fibres with a spot of liquid celluloid.

The methods described above may not be the best. They have been put forward for the sake of their simplicity, which we consider is a first essential in any elementary treatise on fly-dressing. If the angler is ambitious to achieve perfection he will find these and the subsequent hints to be a sound groundwork which, if thoroughly comprehended, will help him considerably in his more advanced studies. If the simplicity of these methods has reduced the " bogey " of fly-dressing to less overpowering proportions, their lack of finesse is justified.

Hackle Wet Flies

The chief difference between these and the former type lies in the materials used. As the name implies, they are of a type calculated to induce the fly to fish below the surface of the water. To this end, soft hen hackles and absorbent bodies are used.

Speaking generally it would almost be possible to dismiss the subject with these few words but for the fact that there are one or two notable exceptions, so as this happens to be a good opportunity to introduce the new types of body previously mentioned we will start with a Cochybondhu. Incidentally this fly can be dressed wet or dry.

Materials include a length of green or brown tying silk, a frond of bronze peacock herl, a soft furnace hackle (i.e., a hackle with an almost black centre and red-brown tips) and a very small piece of flat gold tinsel.

Starting as before wind the silk down from head to tail, tying in the hackle *en route*. At the tail, tie in the length of tinsel with two turns of silk in the same manner as the quill of the Blue Upright was fastened. Park the silk temporarily and make three turns *tailwards* with the tinsel, afterwards winding back again to the point where the silk is " parked." Secure the returned end of tinsel with two turns of silk. Immediately following this little golden tip fasten in the frond of peacock herl, which remains in this position while the silk is wound back to the position just behind the hackle. The fly now looks like Fig. 72A, the positions of the various materials being clearly shown.

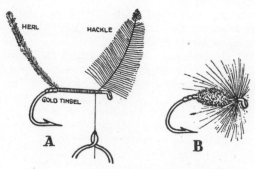

FIG. 72.   A BODY OF PEACOCK HERL

Weight the silk at the head with hackle pliers and pro‐ceed to wind the herl in close coils towards the hackle. It will be seen that the herl so coiled has a metallic sheen which is reminiscent of the body of a beetle, which, in fact, this fly is supposed to represent.

When the coils of herl eventually reach the hackle they are tied in and the surplus cut away. The rest of the process, the tying in of the hackle, etc., has already been described, but there is one slight difference. The hackle on wet flies is usually tied so that it slopes backwards away from the hook ; it does not stand out at right-angles as does the hackle of a dry fly. This effect is obtained by coiling on the head binding close up to the root of the hackle fibres, thus forcing these back away from the eye.

Thus we have another body material. Peacock herl can be obtained in bronze and green shades and is suitable for both wet and dry flies. Other popular patterns on which it appears are Alder, Coachman, Red Tag, Red Ant, etc.

*   *   *   *   *

There is a very popular series of hackle flies known as the Palmers, which are dressed by quite a different method from those hitherto described.   There are at least eight different colour schemes, most popular among which are Black, Brown, Red and Soldier Palmers.   The most suitable for our purpose is the first mentioned.

The tying-silk is black, and so are the hackles, which, in the case of the wet fly, should be soft.   Black wool is the usual material for the body with flat gold tinsel for ribbing.

Wax the silk and start as usual one-sixteenth of an inch behind the eye of the hook.   Lay on a close binding from here to the tail but do not fasten in the hackle on the way down.   At the end of the body thus started tie in a couple of whisks to form the tail.   Take your hackle (which should be short in the fibre but long-stemmed, and not trimmed as heretofore), hold it by the point and brush down the fibres.   Tie in the *point* of the hackle at the tail of the fly with the usual two or three turns of silk.

Next fasten in lengths of black wool and gold tinsel, after which the silk can be rewound to the head of the fly.   At this stage the fly is shown in Fig. 73A.

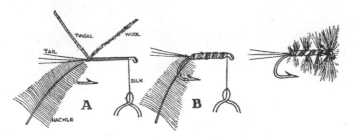

FIG. 73.   DRESSING A " PALMER "

First take the wool and wind it closely towards the head, at which point secure it and cut away the surplus.   Then comes the tinsel which is laid on in open coils so that the black and gold effect is like the colours on a barber's pole.

Secure the tinsel under the tying-silk at the head and trim off.   Take the hackle in the pliers and wind it on in open coils close up to the tinsel ribbing ; when the head is reached tie in as usual. Thus in the Palmer series the hackle runs all the way along the body.

Winged Wet Flies

A popular loch fly, the Grouse and Green, provides a good example of the type in hand. Before starting we shall require to place the following materials in readiness—green silk, bright green seal's fur and gold ribbing for the body ; a soft hackle of green or ginger ; three fibres from a golden pheasant tippet for the tail ; and a pair of grouse wings. The latter should be from the same bird if possible, but in any case they must be left and right wings.

Portions of these are used in making the wing of the fly, and as there is a certain amount of preparation before they are ready for use, it is a good plan to do this before starting to tie the fly.

Take a feather from each wing from corresponding positions. Those we require are the long flight feathers which extend fanwise when the bird is in the air. It will

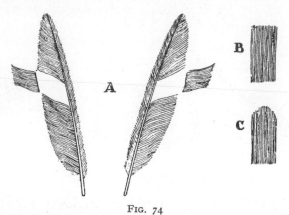

Fig. 74

Showing how the " wings " are extracted from the feather, and the shape to which they are dressed.

be seen that these are the direct opposites of each other, but each has a row of long fibres on one side of the stem, while on the other side the fibres are short. From the

longer side of each feather extract about a quarter of an
inch of fibres as shown in Fig. 74A, taking great care
that these are not ruffled or separated in the process of
extraction.   Scissors are used for this purpose.

Taking each piece separately hold between the first
finger and thumb of *both* hands and " work " the fibres into
shape B—a delicate process this, and one which will spoil
the feather unless great care is exercised.   Still dealing
with each piece separately, stroke into the final shape C.
A moistened finger and thumb will help to persuade the
feather into the shape shown.   For the first time the two
pieces can be placed together, one over the other so that
they fit.   If they show a tendency to form an angle between
themselves it is a sign that the wrong surfaces have been
put together.   Change them around so that they lie snugly.

For the time being we shall not require these wings, but
as they will be blown away on the least current of air it is
advisable to stow them in a safe place.

Now for the actual fly.   Put the hook in the vice and
wind a length of well-waxed green silk from head to tail ;
but do not insert the hackle *en route*.   At the tail tie in the
fibres of Golden Pheasant tippet with two turns of silk.
Tie in also a length of gold braid as close to the tail as
possible.

The body of this fly is made by the process known as
" dubbing," the first step of which is to spin the green
seal's fur on to the tying silk which is hanging from the
tail end of the hook, a proceeding which necessitates
plenty of wax adhering to the silk.

Hold the silk out taut with the left hand and take a
small tuft of seal's fur between the finger and thumb of
the right.   Starting close up to the hook, pinch this on to
the silk and rub the finger and thumb together so that
the fur is worked on to the silk.   Do not try to put too
much on at a time.   The secret of success is to work with
a small quantity (Fig. 75A).

When the fur has been worked on to a sufficient length
of silk the body can be formed by coiling the latter back
towards the eye.   Leave the usual margin at the head of
the hook and if necessary remove surplus fur by drawing
between the finger and thumb nails.

H

Park your silk in the hackle pliers and proceed to make open coils of gold tinsel from the tail forwards. Fasten this in with two turns and a half hitch at the head and trim away the surplus (Fig. 75B).

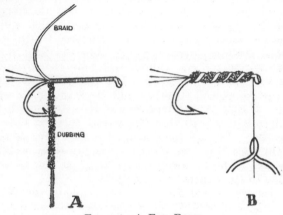

FIG. 75.   A FUR BODY

The fur is dubbed on to the silk and then wound on to the hook.
The braid is then " ribbed " over it.

The hackle should be a soft hen feather and should be treated as shown in Fig. 69, i.e. held by the tip in the hackle pliers and the fibres brushed downwards. Lay the point against the head of the hook and secure with two turns of silk and the usual half hitch. Make three turns of hackle round the hook, bind in the end and cut away the surplus. The appearance of the fly at this stage is similar to the hackle patterns previously described. It is usual, however, on winged wet flies, to bring the hackle down below the hook. Moisten the first finger and thumb of the left hand and stroke all the hackles down below hook-level, in which position hold them while taking a diagonal turn of silk over the top hackles. The word " diagonal " is used to express the idea of the silk running *over* the hook at an angle of 45° or less, in such a manner that the top hackles are held down by it without in any way interfering with those at the bottom

(Fig. 76).   Secure this diagonal turn with a half hitch of silk and the fly is ready for winging.

Take the prepared wing between the first finger and thumb of the left hand, the rounded end of the feather being furthest from the finger tips, and the square end projecting only very slightly there-from.   Place the wing over the hook shank while still compressed between the fingers.   Bring one turn of silk over the finger tips and, keeping a tight line, gradually slide it down and over the feather so that this is pulled down to the shank.   If a strain is kept on the silk the fingers can now be removed to see that the wing is " sitting pretty."   It should look

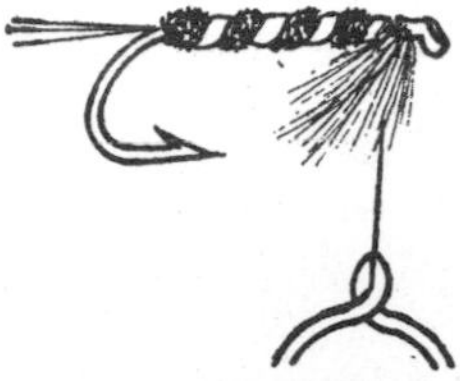

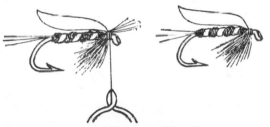

FIG. 76.   HACKLES ON WINGED WET FLIES ARE BROUGHT BELOW THE HOOK

FIG. 77.   WINGING A WET FLY

like Fig. 77.   If it is at all unbalanced it should be readjusted before proceeding further.

The surplus wing which overhangs the head can be cut away with scissors, after which a secure binding of four or six turns completes the fly.   Add a spot of varnish to the head and also a drop of liquid celluloid to the tips of the wings.   The latter will give great protection against the ravages wrought by use.

Winged Dry Flies

By now the reader should have a fair idea of the principles of fly-tying, which should stand him in good stead in his attempts to make the present variety.   The process of body-building on winged dry flies is not materially different from the methods already discussed. The wings, however, present a little problem of their own. Four plies of feather are used in their construction and must result in a correctly cocked, natural-looking artificial. In order that the first effort shall not tax the reader's patience unduly we will tie a very simple form of Black Gnat.

The usual body for this fly is made of black ostrich herl, but an alternative dressing can be effected with black silk, and the latter will present less complication when tying-in the wings and hackle.

Other materials include a right and left feather from a starling's wings, and two black cock hackles.

Before starting on the actual fly we will prepare the wings against the time when they are wanted. Remove pieces of fibre from the feathers in the manner shown in Fig. 74, and dress them up to a width of $\frac{3}{8}$ inch each and of the shape shown. This corresponds to the stage shown in

FIG. 78.   PREPARING THE WINGS OF A DRY FLY

Fig. 78A. The dotted line in this illustration shows that the fibres of each feather should be separated down the middle with a needle, and the resultant halves laid over each other as in B. If these are pressed firmly together they will adhere. Now place the left and right wings together by their roots so that, when viewed head-on, they form the angle shown in C. In this position they are eventually tied to the hook; but as we have not yet reached that stage we will stow the feathers away until required.

Place your hook in the vice and wind a coil of black tying silk from head to tail, not forgetting to leave the usual space just below the eye. (This space is left no matter what type of fly is being tied.) The Black Gnat has no tail whisks so we now wind back again towards the head, thus forming a silk body. Park your silk in the hackle pliers.

Take the two wing feathers between the finger and thumb of the left hand and lay them over the shank. Pass a turn of silk over the fingers and gradually slide this down until it is holding the butt of the feathers to the shank of the hook. Easing the fingers slightly take two more turns around

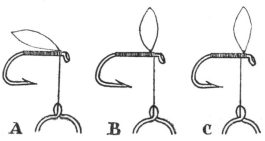

FIG. 79.   WINGING A DRY FLY.

feather and hook.   Cut away the surplus butt of feather. This stage is shown in Fig. 79A.

Lift up the wings as shown in B and make a turn of silk around the hook close behind them, followed by three turns around the *wings themselves* just above where they join the hook.   These turns help to keep the wings cocked. Bring the silk round in another turn in front of the wings then one just behind, ending in a half-hitch in the latter position (Fig. 79C).

Prepare the hackles as in Fig. 69A and B, and tie in the butt ends together just behind the wings with three turns of silk and a half hitch. Snip away the surplus ends.   (Fig. 80A).

Take the point of one hackle and wind a single turn around the hook in front of the wings, then wrap the rest of the hackle around the hook *behind* and close to the wings.   Tie in with silk and snip away the sur-

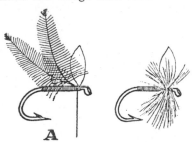

FIG. 80.   ATTACHING THE HACKLE.

plus tip.   Take the other hackle and wrap the whole of it behind the wings and tie in as before with two turns and a half hitch.

Bring your silk forward through the wings and form a head of four or six turns just below the eye. Dab a little celluloid varnish on the tips of the wings, and a little shellac on the head. The fly is now complete.

Perhaps the reader has noticed already that the order of the processes of winging and hackle-tying are reversed in wet and dry flies. In the former the hackle is tied in first and is followed by the wings. In a dry fly the wings are fitted first and the hackles last.

Nymphs.

The growing popularity of nymph fishing is sufficient justification for including simple instructions for dressing these fascinating lures. They represent the immature fly which spends the earlier stages of its career under water. They are thus fished " wet," carry no wings, and very little hackle.

The main anatomical features of the nymph are the head, thorax, abdomen, wing cases, legs, and setae. Some styles of dressing include elaborate wing cases made of selected feathers, and bodies most carefully dressed to a pattern involving the use of several materials.

Such photographic exactitude in the imitation is quite unnecessary. A wonderfully lifelike representation can be made from seal's fur dyed to a dull olive shade, natural mole's fur, a tiny olive hackle, three tail whisks of the same colour, and some pale yellow silk. Most of the materials are easily obtained, but the hackle should be selected with the utmost care. It should be as small as possible and very soft fibred.

Place the hook in the vice and wax a length of the silk. Commencing just behind the eye of the hook wind on the silk in close even turns until a point directly above the barb is reached. Here insert the three tail whisks in the usual manner. They must be quite short—a fraction shorter than the proposed length of the body.

Working back towards the head secure the whisks with three or four turns of silk. These stages are covered by sketches A and B in Fig. 81. Spin a very light dubbing of olive-coloured seal's fur on to the hanging silk (C) and commence winding towards the head. This winding should end at a point slightly more than half way between the end of the body and the eye of the hook (D).

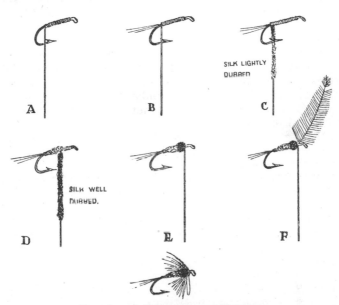

FIG. 81. A DRESSING FOR NYMPHS

Remove the remaining olive seal's fur by drawing the silk between the finger nails. In its place spin on a fairly heavy dubbing of mole's fur. This also is shown in D. This fur is again wound headwards so that it forms a compact round pad of slightly greater diameter than the rest of the body. Being much darker than the olive-coloured fur (the abdomen) this forms a very natural-looking thorax surmounted by wing cases. Secure this pad with a half hitch after removing the surplus fur (E).

Take the hackle and secure it with a couple of turns of silk close in front of the mole's fur, then make three or four turns of hackle round the hook shank. Secure the end, cut away the surplus, and end with a whip finish. Then varnish the head and the nymph is complete.

As will be seen from the sketches, the body tapers away towards the tail. This is a very desirable feature as it closely resembles the shape of the body in the natural insect. This effect can be obtained by a judicious use of the seal's fur.

Mayflies

Mayflies are made in hackled and winged types. The former are tied in exactly the same way as the hackled flies previously described, their only difference lying in the materials used. The winged variety however, call for a little extra attention.

The wings are usually formed from whole breast feathers, dyed or undyed, of the mallard. These are tied in by the butt or quill end at the " shoulder " of the fly so that a V is formed between them. A perfectly balanced and natural setting is very necessary if the fly is to alight and float correctly.

Another refinement on the Mayfly lies in the addition of one or two turns of peacock herl at the head. This is wound in by just the same process as used for butts of salmon flies. Several effective dressings will be found in the following section.

Variations in the standard patterns of trout flies are produced in many ways to suit certain localities. The Test angler would probably scorn the scantily dressed flies of the North. So, likewise, might the Test trout. To put all these slight differences into print would take up too much valuable space. The average angler is sufficiently well acquainted with his own requirements, and is sufficiently well endowed with common sense, to be able to adapt the foregoing information to his own purpose.

We have dealt with the popular body and wing formations in such a manner that the reader should now be in a position to apply his knowledge to the dressing of a vast range of flies. If perchance he desires something a little different to the usual standard, we have no doubt that his present knowledge will help him in achieving his desire. If not we must recommend him to one or other of the excellent books devoted entirely to the subject, which contain much more detail than we could possibly include in a single chapter.

A Few Popular Patterns of Trout Flies

Note :—Where alternative materials are given the first-mentioned is preferable.

(1) *Alder*
> Body : Bronze peacock herl
> Wings : Brown mottled hen or bustard.
> Hackle : Brownish red or black.

(2) *Black Gnat*
> See text.

(3) *Black Spider*
> See text.

(4) *Blue Dun*
> Body : Smoke-grey seal's fur.
> Wings : Starling or snipe wing.
> Hackle : Grey dun cock (dyed).
> Tail : As hackle (three whisks).

(5) *Blue Upright*
> See text.

(6) *Blue-Winged Olive*
> Body : Olive green floss silk.
> Wings : Wing feather from teal or coot.
> Hackle : Medium olive cock.
> Tail : As hackle (Three whisks).

(7) *Butcher*
> Body : Flat silver tinsel.
> Wings : Blue-black feather from drake's wing.
> Hackle : Black.
> Tail : Red ibis.

(8) *Coachman*
> Body : Peacock herl (bronze or green).
> Wings : White.
> Hackle : Red cock.

(9) *Cochybondhu*
> See text.

(10) *February Red*
> Body : Light hare's ear with two turns of claret wool at tail.
> Wings : Palest part of hen pheasant's wing.
> Hackle : Claret.

(11) *Grannom*

    Body : Blue heron's herl with two turns of green floss-silk at tail.

    Wings : Partridge wing feather or pheasant

    Hackle : Ginger.

(12) *Greenwell's Glory*

    Body : Light yellow tying silk ribbed with gold wire.

    Wings : Dark starling or hen blackbird wing.

    Hackle : Furnace.

(13) *Grouse Series*

These are a famous series of wet flies tied to the formula given in the text.   Standard features are a wing made from the tail or wing feather of a grouse, and a ·tail made of golden pheasant tippet.   The body and hackle are of seal's fur and hen hackle respectively but may be of any of the following shades :—black, blue, brown, claret, green, grey, orange, purple, red or yellow, and ribbed with gold or silver wire.

(14) *Iron Blue*

    Body : Natural mole's fur dubbed on red silk.   The last third of the body should be naked red silk.

    Wings : Starling wing dyed blue dun.

    Hackle : Rusty-red.

    Tail : As hackle.

(15) *Mallard Series*

As Grouse series except that wings are bronze breast feathers from a mallard.

(16) *March Brown*

    Body : Hare's ear mixed claret wool and ribbed with yellow silk.

    Wings : Hen pheasant's wing or tail feather.

    Hackle : Brown partridge back feather.

    Tail : As hackle.

(17a) *Mayfly*

    Body : White floss silk, ribbed black tying silk.

    Wings : Grey mallard breast feathers dyed pale green.

    Hackle : Cock's hackle also dyed pale green.

    Tail : Three black whisks.

(17b) *Mayfly*
> Body : As above.
> Wings : Grey mallard (undyed).
> Hackle : Badger.
> Tail : As above.

(17c) *Mayfly*
> Body : Raffia, ribbed black silk.
> Wings : Grey Mallard breast (natural).
> Hackle : Ginger cock's.
> Tail : As above.

(17d) *Mayfly*
> Body : Pale green seal's fur, ribbed dark green tying silk.
> Wings : Teal breast, dyed pale green.
> Hackle : Inner of soft wing feather of a woodcock. Outer of cock's hackle dyed pale green.

(17e) *Mayfly*
> Body : Raffia grass, ribbed black silk.
> Hackle : Medium olive.
> Tail : As hackle.

(17f) *Spent Gnat*
> Body : Raffia grass, ribbed brown horsehair.
> Wings : Natural or dyed blue dun hackle points, set horizontally.
> Hackle : Dark grouse, at head ; pale yellow cock's at shoulder.
> Tail : Three dark brown whisks.

(18) *Palmer series*
A hackle fly dressed as in text but in a wide variety of body colours.

(19) *Red Sedge*
> Body : Dark red wool, ribbed gold wire or tinsel.
> Wings : Brown partridge tail feather.
> Hackle : Red cock's, dressed as Palmer, i.e., all along body.

(20) *Red Spinner*
> Body : Red floss silk, ribbed silver.
> Wings : Starling or snipe.
> Hackle : Red cock's.
> Tail : As hackle.

(21) *Snipe series*

A hackle fly dressed in all the body colours of the Grouse series. The body is formed of tying silk and the hackle is the same throughout, i.e., the small wing feather of a snipe, tied sparsely.

(22) *Spider series*

Tied as per Black Spider but with a variety of hackle and body colours.

(23) *Teal series*

Throughout the series the standard features are a wing formed of teal breast feathers and a tail of golden pheasant tippet. Otherwise as grouse.

(24) *Wickham's Fancy*

>Body : Alternate ribbings of flat gold tinsel and red cock hackle.
>
>Wing : Starling wing.
>
>Hackle : Red cock.
>
>Tail : As hackle.

(25) *Woodcock series*

Woodcock wing feather and tail of golden pheasant tippet. Otherwise as grouse.

Materials and equipment for Salmon Flies

The reader who purchases the fly-tying tools illustrated in Fig. 67 and recommended for trout flies, will find that they are in every way suitable for the dressing of flies for salmon. No alterations or additions are necessary.

It is a pity that this cannot also be said of the materials. If such were possible a great financial saving could be effected. It is indeed unfortunate that so few trout-fly materials are embodied in salmon flies, and that the variety of salmon-fly materials is so wide and so costly.

As in trout fly dressing, the angler can save money by tying his own flies providing that he does not try to acquire too ambitious a collection of materials. Books on salmon fishing have repeated *ad nauseam* that the size of the fly is of much greater importance than the colour. This seems to indicate that the wise man is he who concentrates on a few well-chosen dressings tied in a wide variety of sizes. The angler of modest means will welcome such a suggestion with open arms, as by adopting it he can save considerably on his initial outlay for materials.

At the end of this chapter is given a list of twelve salmon flies with instructions for dressing. These should be sufficient for any but the most fastidious ; and providing that they are tied in several sizes they will yield as many fish as if their variety were trebled.

This suggestion may not be acceptable to certain anglers, and to those who can afford to do so there is no reason why they should not indulge their every whim as far as flies are concerned. For these last, the list of materials which follows these remarks will be found sufficiently comprehensive to cover a much wider variety of flies than the dozen given at the end of the chapter ; but the thrifty angler is advised to make an analysis of the materials used in the said dozen, and to commence his fly-dressing with these only.

*   *   *   *   *

Hackles consist of natural cock-hackles in grizzled, cochybondhu, badger, furnace, red and black ; and dyed cock hackles in turquoise or pale blue, scarlet, claret, orange, lemon, hot brown, green and olive. Badger hackles, the natural colour of which is a black centre with a white tip, should be obtained dyed in the following shades : — lemon, red and hot brown.

Hackles are also formed of the feathers taken from the sides of the bodies of Teal, Widgeon and Summer Duck ; from the breast of Grouse, Partridge, Gallina and Golden Pheasant ; from the rump of Grouse, Partridge, Gallina, Snipe and Woodcock ; from the back of Golden Pheasant, Woodcock and Gallina ; and blue feathers of the Jay. In addition a few Spey-cock hackles in natural shades are fairly useful.

Wings are formed from feathers taken from Teal, Mallard, Widgeon, Summer Duck, Bustard (wing and tail), Golden Pheasant, Peacock (wing), Pheasant (tail), and Turkey cock (tail).

Dyed feathers for wings in orange, lemon, blue, red and green are also popular.

Other feathers include Indian Crow (breast), Blue Chatterer, Jungle Cock, Toucan (breast), black Ostrich herl, Peacock herl, and Macaw (tail).

Bodies consist of floss silk, Seal's fur, and Berlin wools, dyed orange, lemon, light blue, hot brown, green, olive, scarlet, claret and black ; and ribbings for same are made of gold and silver tinsel (flat and wire).

This completes the list of materials with the exception of tying silk (any neutral colour) and hooks. The latter should be finest quality eyed Limericks, strong in the wire and needle-sharp, ranging in size from 6 to 3/0. Larger or smaller sizes are used under certain circumstances but the above range covers all the popular sizes.

Bodies of Salmon Flies

When dealing with trout flies we found it simpler to choose an example of each of the leading types and to use it as an illustration of the method of dressing. To apply the same method to salmon flies would be impracticable owing to the wide variety of styles in which they are dressed. We propose, therefore, to divide the operation into two sections—body-dressing and wing-dressing.

The terms " body " and " wing " are here used in a rather loose sense to denote the collection of materials which form the *ensemble* of the respective parts.

In Fig. 82 we have a rough sketch of an imaginary salmon fly. It will be noted that the parts of the fly come under

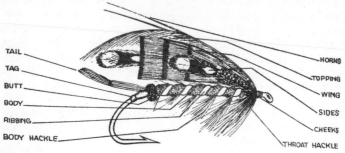

FIG. 82.   SALMON FLY DISSECTED

twelve different headings. Actually all these parts do not occur in every fly, but the one shown has been chosen to make the reader familiar with the names of the various features. As mentioned already, we propose to divide these under the headings of " body " and " wing."

The body section will include, in addition to the actual body itself, the tag, butt, tail, ribbing and body hackle. The wing section will include throat hackle, wings, sides, cheeks, horns and topping. A glance at the illustration will identify the various parts.

* * * * *

Place the hook in the vice and make a close binding of well-waxed tying silk from the head to the bend, but as usual leave a little space just below the eye for finishing off.

The first body part to be inserted is the Tag. This may be made of tinsel, floss silk or wool ; or a combination of the first-mentioned with either of the latter. If only one material is used the end is tied in under two turns of tying silk. The latter is temporarily " parked " and the tag material is wound tailwards round the shank until it reaches a point directly over the barb of the hook. It is then wound back over the first coil and is tied in when it reaches the tying silk. The surplus is cut away and the fly is ready to receive the tail.

It is usual to tie in the Tail and the Butt simultaneously, or at any rate the butt is tied in before the tail is trimmed away. Most tails are made from Golden Pheasant topping which is frequently augmented by the use of Golden Pheasant tippet, Indian Crow breast feathers, dyed Swan feathers or red Ibis. These last usually occupy about half the length of the topping and serve the double purpose of giving it support and additional colour.

Butts are made from Ostrich or Peacock herl (dyed or natural) or wool dyed in a variety of shades.

Our last turn of silk was used to tie in the tag ; our next turn is used to secure the tail. See that the topping forms a graceful upward curve as is usual in salmon flies. The following turn, working towards the head, is used to tie in the end of the butt after which a further three turns to the right are made with the tying silk. So far the dressing is shown in Fig. 83A.

Park the silk temporarily and make a few close turns around the shank with the butt material, which in our sketch is peacock herl. Wind this so that it forms the little " belt " seen in the following sketch ; bind in the end with tying silk and cut away the surplus tail and butt. Insert the end of the Ribbing tinsel under the following turn. Make six more turns towards the right and " park " the silk.

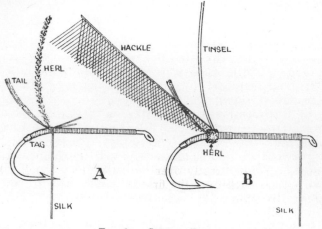

FIG. 83.   SALMON FLY

A = Silk wound on, tag wound on, tail and butt inserted.   B = Butt wound on, tinsel and hackle inserted, and silk returned to head.

Take the Hackle and brush up the fibres as previously described. Then with a moistened thumb and forefinger fold these over as seen in Fig. 83B.

Insert the point of the hackle under the silk and continue winding the latter to the right until the eye is almost reached. Thus we have reached the stage shown in Fig. 83B.

We now come to the Body proper, which may be formed either of fur, floss silk or tinsel. For the present example we will use floss silk.

The end of the floss silk is tied in at the head as shown in Fig. 84A, i.e., with the short end pointing tailwards. This gives a neater head and also gives taper to the body. Park the tying silk and wind the floss tailwards as far as the butt, taking care not to trap the hackle *en route*. Wind the floss back again to the head thus forming a second coil over the first and tie in at the starting point. Snip away the surplus.

Now take the ribbing tinsel and wind it in evenly-laid open turns. As before, tie in when the head is reached and trim away.

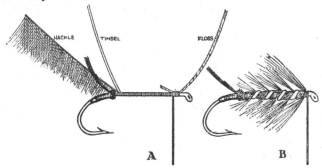

FIG. 84.   SALMON FLY
A = Floss silk inserted.   B = Finished body.

The hackle comes next and is wound on and secured in just the same way as the tinsel, each layer lying close behind the preceding layer of ribbing. Thus the body is complete (Fig. 84B).

If fur is used the procedure is not materially different. After the butt is tied in, the hackle is inserted close up to it. The fur is dubbed on to the silk at this point and is wound headwards, where the silk is parked. The ribbing and hackle follow as before.

*   *   *   *   *

The body described embodies all the main features usually seen in dressings of salmon flies, but many patterns do not include all these features. The body itself is common to all, and in almost every case is ribbed with tinsel or other material. Tails are fairly general but are omitted from some dressings including most of the Spey flies. There are many flies where butts and tags do not occur as is again instanced by most Spey dressings. There are also a few (but very few) which have no body hackle.

There are numerous cases where the body proper is formed of more than one variety or colour of material, which may either be wound on in alternate coils like the

I

colours on a barber's pole or, alternatively, in sections. As an example of the latter we have flies such as the Jock Scott, which has a lemon coloured body for the tail half and black for the head half ; or the Popham, whose body is divided into thirds, showing red, yellow, and blue from tail to head, with a coil of herl, tied butt-wise, between each section ; or again the Dreadnought, whose body is mainly silver tinsel with tufts of seal's fur in scarlet, brown and blue which appear in turn at three equally spaced points from tail to head.

Occasionally hackles are mixed and spaced in a similar manner. The Rosy Dawn for instance has a body divided into halves of gold and silver, and instead of the usual coiled hackle, this is wound on in a " belt " between the two tinsels, and again at the head.

The wingless flies, known as grubs, offer several examples of the " belt " style of hackle and body dressing. The body may be divided into two or three sections of similar or contrasting materials and the hackles, again matching or contrasting, are inserted in belts between the sections of body. This style calls for a slightly different procedure from that previously mentioned, but the requirements will be obvious once the general idea of fly-dressing is grasped.

Wings of Salmon Flies

In winging trout flies the chief difficulty lies in making a neat job of so small a wing, though the materials employed are usually very simple. This cannot be said of salmon flies for, though the wing is large enough to facilitate handling, the materials used are far from simple, embodying as they do, so many separate pieces of feather. (It must be understood that the word " wing " here applies to the whole wing assembly.)

The simplest style is known as the strip-wing. The body is made first in whichever style is appropriate to the fly under construction, and the tying silk lies parked at the head, awaiting further orders.

The most popular material for strip-winged patterns is the tail feather of a Pheasant. Sections of this are extracted from opposite feathers (left and right) in a similar fashion to that illustrated in Fig. 74, but instead of cutting out a section of fibre with the scissors we must now use a knife ; and instead of removing the fibre by severing the roots, we free it by slicing away the strip of quill into which it is rooted. (Fig. 85). It is important that the sections be extracted from opposite feathers, and that they match exactly in length and width.

FIG. 85. FEATHERS EXTRACTED TO FORM WING

Lay the two pieces back to back and hold between the first finger and thumb of the left hand. Lay these over the body of the fly in such a position that their tips extend backwards over the hook to a point just beyond the bend. Bring the tying silk over just in front of the finger and thumb and secure the wing with two turns. (Fig. 86.) Release the feather and see if it is sitting correctly. If not, unwind the silk and repeat the process.

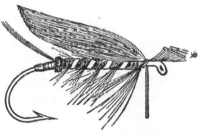

FIG. 86. TYING IN THE WING

When satisfactory, the surplus ends are cut away and the head is finished with whipping and varnish (Fig. 87).

That sounds very simple ; in fact the strip-wing offers less difficulty than that of a trout fly. It is certainly the simplest of salmon fly wings because it consists of a single material and is not usually decorated with other features of wing-assembly.

FIG. 87. FINISHED FLY

*   *   *   *

A more complicated dressing, which is found with slight variations on many salmon ·flies, is that used for the

Rangers. It is built up of three pairs of feathers, plus cheeks, topping, horns, etc., where these are appropriate.

The six feathers which go to form the Wing proper, are two Jungle Cock neck feathers and two *pairs* of feathers from the neck of a Golden Pheasant. Of the latter one pair must be much smaller than the other. Jungle Cock is also very popular for the Sides, as also is Indian Crow. Cheeks may be formed of Blue Chatterer or Indian Crow, but for the Topping, Golden Pheasant's crest is the only material used. The Horns, if any are included, are most commonly taken from the Macaw's tail, and may be obtained in two or three colours.

As regards the Throat Hackle, this may be either the same as the body hackle or contrasting, according to the prescribed pattern. Some flies have a throat hackle of mixed colours ; a result which is obtained by tying in two hackles of different shades.

When the body of the fly is finished the next step is to tie in the Throat Hackle. The tip of the hackle is secured under the tying silk at the head, and the subsequent procedure is identical to that of tying a hackle on a winged wet trout fly. This has already been described so we will pass on to the Wing proper.

Take the larger pair of Jungle Cock feathers and trim away the soft downy fibres at the butt end of the quill ; they are useless for our purpose and will interfere with

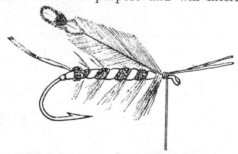

Fig. 88.   Building up the wing—Jungle Cock Feathers inserted

the " set " of the wing. Lay the two feathers back to back and tie them in with two turns of silk and a half-hitch in the position illustrated in Fig. 88, which also shows that the usable length of feather should be about the same length as the hook, or if anything slightly shorter. Do not cut away the surplus quill until later.

Take the two large feathers from the Golden Pheasant and place one each side of the Jungle Cock, allowing the latter to protrude as shown in the next sketch. Tie these in with two turns of silk.

They are followed by the two smaller feathers. Lay these one each side so that there are three dark bars visible

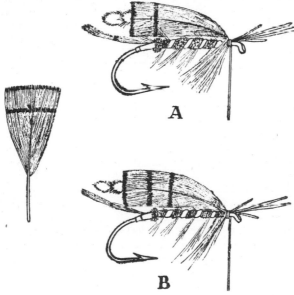

A

B

FIG. 89. BUILDING UP THE WING—TIPPETS INSERTED

(Fig. 89B). Again leave the surplus quill intact. If this is cut away at this stage it makes the tying in of the remaining materials much more difficult and clumsy.

The Sides are tied in next and are followed by the Cheeks, each fresh material being slightly shorter than the preceding one so that when the cheeks are reached they are just a tuft of short fibres extending from the head of the fly.

By this time there are several surplus fibres extending

over the eye of the hook. These should be trimmed away as closely as possible, and any vagrant ends bound in with tying silk.

The Topping—a crest of Golden Pheasant—is carefully selected in a length which will cause it to curve gracefully over the wing of the fly. This is tied in at the head ; the two Horns follow, and the fly is complete except for whipping and varnish.

It is important, while dressing salmon flies, to regularly inspect both sides of the fly during building. See that each is an exact duplicate of the other, a result which is achieved by the careful pairing and setting of the various materials. See also that perfect balance is maintained ; the size of wings and other materials being in proportion to the size of the hook.

*   *   *   *   *

The two types of wing so far mentioned are the most definite styles used on salmon flies. There are several variations, some of which almost qualify as distinct styles of their own. Some for instance, are formed of a collection of fibres and strips which are blended together before tying in, usually over a whole feather which forms a background. The chief difference between these and other dressings is the mixing of the materials, a process which cannot be adequately described on paper though it could be quickly taught by a few minutes of practical demonstration.

We will, therefore, fall back on an earlier statement to the effect that this chapter is intended to be quite elementary and not by any means exhaustive.

Twelve Popular Dressings for Salmon Flies.

(1) *Akroyd*

Tag	-	- Silver.
Tail	-	- Golden Pheasant topping and tippet.
Body	-	- Tail half, orange seal's fur ; then black.
Body Hackle	-	Lemon first half ; then black.
Throat Hackle		Teal.
Wings	-	- White turkey tail strips.
Cheeks	-	- Jungle Cock breast feather.

(2) *Blue Charm.*

Tag	-	- Silver thread and yellow floss silk.
Tail	-	- Golden Pheasant topping.
Butt	-	- Black Ostrich herl.
Body	-	- Black floss silk.
Ribbing	-	- Silver tinsel.
Throat Hackle		Blue.
Wings	-	- Brown Turkey (tail) and a few Teal fibres.
Topping	-	- Golden Pheasant.

(3) *Childers.*

Tag	-	- Silver tinsel and pale blue floss silk.
Tail	-	- Golden Pheasant topping with strands of blue and red Macaw.
Butt	-	- Black Ostrich herl.
Body	-	- Light yellow silk, followed by orange Seal's fur and red Seal's fur.
Ribbing	-	- Silver tinsel.
Body Hackle	-	A white furnace hackle dyed yellow.
Throat Hackle		Scarlet followed by light Widgeon.
Wings	-	- Golden Pheasant tippet, followed by strands of Turkey, Pintail, Summer Duck, Bustard, blue and red Macaw, and Gallina.
Cheeks	-	- Blue Chatterer.
Horns	-	- Blue Macaw.
Topping	-	- Golden Pheasant.

(4) *Durham Ranger.*

Tag	-	- Silver tinsel and light yellow floss.
Tail	-	- Golden Pheasant Topping and Indian Crow.
Butt	-	- Black Ostrich herl.
Body	-	- Yellow floss followed by orange Seal's fur. Black Seal's fur for head half.
Ribbing	-	- Silver tinsel.
Body Hackle	-	Badger dyed orange.
Throat Hackle		Light blue.
Wings	-	- Four Golden Pheasant tippets arranged as in text, enclosing two Jungle Cock breast feathers.

Cheeks   -   - Blue Chatterer.
Horns   -   - Blue Macaw.
Topping -   - Golden Pheasant.

(5) *Jock Scott.*
Tag   -   - Silver tinsel and yellow silk.
Tail   -   - Golden Pheasant topping and Indian Crow.
Butt   -   - Black Ostrich herl.
Body   -   - First half light yellow floss, tufted midway with Toucan. Last half black floss.
Ribbing -   - Silver tinsel.
Body Hackle -   Black, over black floss only.
Throat Hackle   Gallina.
Wings   -   - Two strips of white-tipped black Turkey ; strips of Mallard, Bustard, Peacock, and Swan dyed red, blue and yellow.
Sides   -   - Jungle Cock.
Cheeks   -   - Blue Chatterer.
Horns   -   - Blue Macaw.
Topping -   - Golden Pheasant.

(6) *March Brown.*
Tag   -   - Silver tinsel.
Tail   -   - Summer Duck.
Body   -   - Hare's mask, dubbed on tying silk.
Ribbing -   - Silver tinsel.
Throat Hackle   Partridge back or rump.
Wings   -   - Strips of hen Pheasant tail.

(7) *Mar Lodge.*
Tag   -   - Silver tinsel.
Tail   -   - Golden Pheasant topping and a pair of Jungle Cock feathers.
Butt   -   - Black Ostrich herl.
Body   -   - Silver tinsel, with turn of black floss in middle.
Ribbing -   - Silver wire.
Throat Hackle   Gallina.
Wings   -   - Strands of Golden Pheasant tippet, Bustard, Florican, and white Swan,

Turkey (grey and brown) and
Golden Pheasant tail.

Sides   -   - Barred Summer Duck.
Cheeks -   - Jungle Cock.
Topping -   - Golden Pheasant.
Horns   -   - Blue Macaw.

(8) *Popham*.

Tag   -   - Gold.
Tail   -   - Golden Pheasant topping and Indian
Crow.
Butt   -   - Black Ostrich herl.
Body   -   - Three equal sections. First, orange
floss ending with butt of black
Ostrich herl and tufted with Indian
Crow. Yellow floss also butted and
tufted as before. Light blue floss.
Ribbing -   Gold over first two sections, silver
over blue section.
Throat Hackle Jay.
Wings -   - Golden Pheasant tippet, Golden
Pheasant tail, Teal, Bustard, Gallina,
brown Turkey, red and yellow
Macaw, and Mallard.
Cheeks -   - Blue Chatterer.
Horns   -   - Blue Macaw.

(9) *Silver Doctor*.

Tag   -   - Yellow floss and silver.
Tail   -   - Golden Pheasant topping and Chat-
terer.
Butt   -   - Scarlet herl or wool.
Body   -   - Flat silver tinsel.
Ribbing -   - Silver wire.
Throat Hackle Pale blue and Widgeon.
Wings -   - Golden Pheasant tippet and tail;
strands of scarlet, blue, and yellow
Swan; strands of Turkey tail,
Bustard, Peacock and Florican, and
strips of Teal, Summer Duck and
Mallard.
Topping -   - Golden Pheasant.

(10) *Silver Wilkinson.*

Tag	-	- Silver tinsel.
Tail	-	- Golden Pheasant topping and tippet.
Butt	-	- Scarlet wool.
Body	-	- Flat silver tinsel.
Ribbing -		- Silver wire.
Throat Hackle		Light blue with magenta over.
Wing	-	- Two strips Summer Duck (barred) and fibres of red Macaw ; two long and two short Jungle Cock.
Sides	-	- Short tippet.
Cheeks	-	- Blue Chatterer.
Horns	-	- Blue and yellow Macaw.

(11) *Spring Grub.*

Tag	-	- Silver twist and light blue floss.
Tail	-	- Strips of red Ibis and blue Macaw.
Butt	-	- Furnace hackle dyed orange.
Body	-	- Tail half, bright yellow floss, second half, black floss.
Ribbing -		- Over yellow floss, black wool ; over black floss, silver tinsel.
Body Hackle -		Blue Gallina wound on in a " belt " between the two halves of the body.
Throat Hackle		Natural Cochybondu and Gallina dyed orange.

(12) *Thunder and Lightning.*

Tag	-	- Golden yellow floss and silver.
Tail	-	- Golden Pheasant topping and Indian Crow.
Butt	-	- Black Ostrich herl.
Body	-	- Black floss silk.
Ribbing -		- Gold tinsel.
Body Hackle -		Orange.
Throat Hackle		Jay.
Wings	-	- Strips of brown Mallard.
Cheeks	-	- Jungle Cock.
Topping -		- Golden Pheasant.
Horns	-	- Blue and yellow Macaw.

V

HOOK TACKLES

UNDER this general heading we propose to deal with those hook tackles, from plain hooks-to-gut to pike snaps, etc., which have not already been dealt with under the heading of spinning tackles. They comprise some of the least expensive items of angling equipment if bought from the tackle shop, but despite this a saving can be effected by making them at home.

In the building of these tackles the reader will find that the tiny vice, mentioned in "Fly Dressing," is a great asset; it will hold hooks securely, thus leaving both hands free for the manipulation of other materials—a boon to unprofessional fingers.

Materials are very simple; hooks and trebles, etc., must be purchased according to the tackles in hand; also gut, wire, or gimp. Common to all are tying silk, cobbler's wax and celluloid or shellac varnish; a useful extra is a spool of thin plated copper-wire.

Cobbler's wax is often difficult to work when in the solid form. A good plan is to obtain a small bottle into which a quantity of the fragments of wax should be placed. Fill up the bottle with methylated spirit and cork up securely. After some time the wax will dissolve into the spirit. More wax should be added from time to time until no more will dissolve; the liquid is then ready for use. In this form the dressing is readily absorbed by the silk and is very effective in use.

Celluloid varnish can be made at home also, but it would be foolish to pretend that the home-made product is as good as the bought variety; nevertheless it is quite a good substitute and very inexpensive to produce. Cut up a number of thin strips of clear celluloid and place these in a small jar with a screw stopper. Pour over them sufficient amylacetate to barely cover them, replace the stopper and allow the celluloid to dissolve. More celluloid should be added until the solution will hold no more. The varnish is then ready for use. Remember to keep the lid tightly screwed as amylacetate evaporates very rapidly if exposed to the air.

The chief objection to the home-made product is that it has not much " body." This can be overcome by applying several coats; it dries within a few minutes of being applied, so there is very little delay.

Hooks to Gut.

The first process to learn, in the making of hook tackles, is that of binding hooks to gut. It is employed in almost every variety of this class of tackle and its usefulness, as a neat and effective union, cannot be over-estimated. All uneyed hooks, and some eyed, are attached by the same method even though there are occasional differences in the materials used.

An ordinary uneyed river or sea hook is attached in the following way.

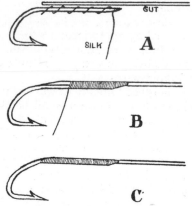

FIG. 90.   SECURING UNEYED HOOK TO GUT

Place the hook in the vice with the shank pointing to the right. (If the angler does not possess a vice he should have no difficulty in managing without.) Take a short length of natural undyed silk, wax it well, and make a few tight but spaced turns over the hook as in Fig. 90A. Lay the gut along the shank of the hook (also shown in illustration) and, starting at the point of the shank, commence to wind towards the bend, pulling the silk as taut as possible.

Continue winding in close, even coils until two thirds of the shank are covered. Temporarily park the silk at this stage and proceed to scrape gently at the exposed tail of gut in such a way that it tapers off towards the end (B). A sharp knife makes quite an efficient parer, but it must be used with discretion. If undue force is applied, too much gut will be removed, thus weakening the tackle. When a suitable degree of taper has been obtained pick up the silk again and continue binding. Secure at the tail with a whip finish and give the binding at least one coat of celluloid or shellac varnish.

Exactly the same method is used for making the Pennel and Stewart tackles shown in Fig. 91, except that the gut-

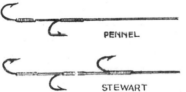

FIG. 91. PENNELL AND STEWART TACKLES

tapering process applies only to the bottom hook. These patterns are much used in worm-fishing for trout.

* * * * *

Eyed hooks can be secured by a binding in addition to forming a knot in the gut, thus obtaining double security. The gut must first be soaked to soften it. Pass the end through the eye of the hook and form a simple half hitch round the shank, but leave a short length of gut protruding

FIG. 92. SECURING EYED HOOK TO GUT

from the knot and running towards the bend (Fig. 92A). Pull the knot tight and close up to the eye, and bind down the end of gut to the shank in the usual way (B). This is by far the neatest and strongest way of attaching eyed hooks to gut.

The method of attachment shown in Fig. 92 can also be applied to Pennel and Stewart tackles. Small eyed hooks are used ; these are attached, in twos or threes, according to the type of tackle, to a length of gut. The gut is passed through the eye of the hook, a half-hitch is tied round the shank, and a binding follows. The second hook is tied on in a similar manner half an inch above the first ; but when working upwards it will be found necessary to tie the half hitch round the shank first, and pass the end of gut through the eye afterwards. This style of tackle is a little bulkier than if uneyed hooks are used, but it is very secure.

Several methods of tying gut to eyed hooks without binding are shown in the chapter on knots.

Uneyed double or treble hooks, no matter whether secured to gut, gimp, or wire, are attached by a similar method. First taper the tail end of the gut. Lay the main length along the shank and pass the tapered end between the " legs " and double it back, along the shank. Bind as before with well-waxed silk, and finish off with varnish (see Fig. 93).

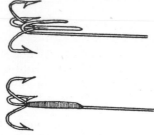

FIG. 93.   ATTACHING UNEYED TREBLES TO GUT OR GIMP

A quite satisfactory method of attaching trebles is to proceed as before but using thin copper wire (fuse wire) instead of silk. To the novice it is much more manageable and can be finished off by twisting the two ends of wire together and neatly stowing away. Thus the whip finish is eliminated. This method has many advantages when building up small minnow tackles for trout fishing.

* * * * *

Nothing has so far been said about the loop at the other end of the hook length. This can be made in four ways. The first is to form a loop by using one of the appropriate knots mentioned in the chapter on that subject. Another simple method is to fold the gut into a loop and whip the end to the main length. The end is folded over and a few loose twists are made round the main length which is followed by a close binding of waxed natural silk and finished by varnishing. This method is practically standardized on most sizes of river hooks. It has the advantage of being

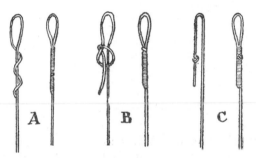

FIG. 94. HOW TO FORM LOOPS IN GUT OR GIMP

very neat but cannot be subjected to very great strains (Fig. 94A).

A stronger union is effected by knotting the gut as in **B** and whipping the protruding end to the main length.

Another method is that illustrated in C. A single half-hitch knot is tied in the gut a short distance from the end. The knot is pulled tight and the gut is folded over as shown. The two lengths are then bound together *above* and *below* the knot. Even if this loop slips (an unlikely event) it still remains intact.

* * * * *

The use of *eyed* trebles to gut or gimp is recommended only when fishing for very heavy game fish. However, as they are sometimes useful under other circumstances, the attachments shown in Fig. 95 are well worth noting.

The foregoing remarks should be quite sufficient to enable the reader to make a trustworthy attachment of hook to gut or wire. For this reason they should be carefully

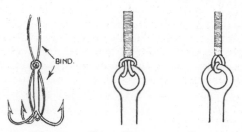

FIG. 95.   ATTACHING EYED TREBLES TO GUT OR GIMP

studied by the angler who intends making any of the spinning tackles mentioned in another chapter. Before leaving the question, however, we will describe the application of these principles to the manufacture of certain other tackles.

Pike Snaps.

The three most popular types of snap tackle for pike fishing are shown in Fig. 96. Type A consists of two hooks (one movable and the other uneyed) of the pattern shown, and a length of twisted rustless wire. The latter should be as soft as possible ; hard springy wire will prevent the bait from working freely.

The uneyed hook is attached to the end·of the wire by the method illustrated in Fig. 93. The other end of the wire is passed through the lower eye of the adjustable hook, wound once or twice round the shank, and brought out through the upper eye. A loop is then formed as shown in Fig. 94. Varnish all bindings and the snap is complete.

If the angler so desires he can make up this tackle with an ordinary treble hook in the lower position. The size varies between 7 and 3.

A suitable tackle for small baits is shown in the following sketch (**B**). It is assembled by just the same method as **A**, but a lip-hook replaces the double hook of the previous pattern.

Type C offers many advantages ; it gives a better balance and support to the bait, which can be much larger than with the previous patterns ; and it is fitted with a hook at both head and tail, thus giving greater hooking power. Materials comprise two trebles, a movable lip hook, and a length of twisted rustless wire.

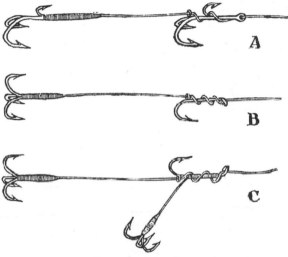

FIG. 96. PIKE SNAPS

A short length of wire is bound to a treble hook and the other end is half-hitched round the shank of the lip hook. The loose end projecting from this half hitch is bound to the shank of the lip hook. A longer piece of wire is bound to the other treble, passed through and around the lip hook, and looped at its top end for attachment to the cast.

The " lip " hook in this instance is used to pass through the dorsal fin of the bait, thus supporting it in the middle ; the other hooks are fixed at the head and tail.

If desired the angler can make his own adjustable hooks. A tiny loop of brass wire (gauge 24) is bound on to the shank

K

of an ordinary hook of the type required. The same principle is illustrated in Fig. 25.

Hook Mounting for Tope Fishing.

Tope tackles, being designed to cope with very heavy fish, are mounted by safer methods than those so far mentioned. The hook may be anything from a 4/0 to an 8/0 according to the fancy of the user or to the size of the bait. The hook length is always of wire, the best of which is the rustless, cable-laid steel wire sold by some tackle manufacturers. Next best is a single strand of rustless wire of gauge 20, though of late many anglers have found that Bowden wire is very satisfactory. The latter, however, is rather thick and may not please the man who prefers to fish fine.

There are two good methods of attaching the first and last mentioned wires. Fig. 97A is self-explanatory. The

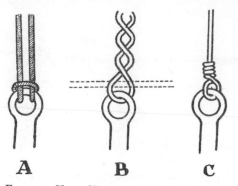

A   B   C

FIG. 97.   HOOK MOUNTING TO HEAVY WIRE

For extra strength the wire in B can be passed twice through the eye before twisting.

short end of wire which projects above the knot should be bound to the main length with thin copper wire, after which it should be covered with a thin coat of solder. In B the wires are twisted *round each other* (not one round the other). Afterwards bind with copper wire and finish with solder. When making B it is important to leave a certain amount of free space in the loop so that there is no restriction to the hook's movement. This can be effected by inserting a thick knitting needle in the loop while the twists are being made. This is shown by dotted lines in the illustration.

The loop system of trace attachment would not be strong enough for tope fishing. The usual procedure is to attach

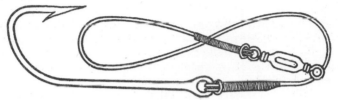

FIG. 98. TOPE HOOK MOUNTED

one end of the wire to the hook (preferably an O'Shaughnessy) and the other end by the same method to a strong swivel as in Fig. 98.

Some anglers prefer large eyed trebles rather than single hooks and these can be attached in exactly the same way.

The best tackle of all, however, comprises a hook and trace in one (as distinct from the detachable type). The trace is two yards long and is divided into thirds, which are united by swivels.

If single strand rustless wire is used the reader will find that the chapter on wirework will give him all the necessary information on forming the loops for hook and swivel attachment. Fig. 97c shows how the loop is applied to the O'Shaughnessy hook, but it should be remembered that this method is unsuitable for attaching the other types of wire.

Mounts for Devon Minnows.

Devons fall into two main types, slotted and slotless, and the mounts vary accordingly. The slotted variety usually carry three trebles, and the mount is forced to revolve with the bait owing to the fact that it is held in position by the slots.

The slotless, on the other hand, has one, or sometimes two, hooks; and the bait revolves on a bead which is threaded on to the shank. Although this does not always work out

perfectly in practice it is nevertheless infinitely superior to
the slotted type, which it is rapidly superseding.   However,
as there are still people who favour the old-fashioned
slotted minnow, we will give details of mounts for both
types.

Hook sizes vary according to the size of the lure, so it is
impossible to give any suggestions in this connection.   The
reader should choose a size which stands well out from the
Devon without being in any way disproportionate.   Gut
or rustless wire can be used according to the strains which
the tackle may be called upon to withstand ; but in either
case it is advisable, as a safeguard against chafing, to double
the material used.

In Fig. 99 we have four types which are suitable for use
on slotless Devons.   They offer a choice of single or treble

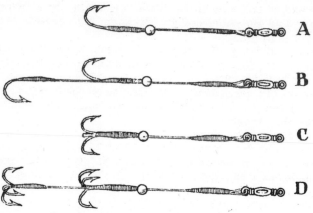

FIG. 99.   MOUNTS FOR SLOTLESS DEVONS

hooks with either single or double mounting.   For minnows
up to one inch in length Type A is preferable, but on the
larger sizes Type C is an easy favourite.   Types B and D
however, are very useful for short rising fish.

There is no need to repeat what is already known about
binding in the hooks.   Secure these to the gut or wire in
the usual way leaving plenty of space for the body length.
When the hooks are fastened in, thread a smooth round

bead from the free end close down on the shank of the foremost. This can be seen in each illustration. Bend over the free end of wire until the distance between the bend and the bead is equivalent to the length of the Devon. Thread a swivel into position and bind the free end to the main length with binding silk. This should be a long binding as shown. It is a good plan to pass the wire twice through the swivel eye.

For slotted Devons carrying three hooks, Types 100A and B are most suitable. The former consists of a large

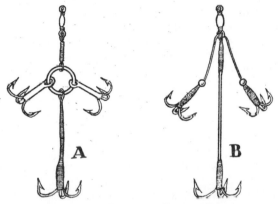

FIG. 100.   MOUNTS FOR SLOTTED DEVONS

split ring which unites two eyed trebles, an uneyed treble, and a swivel. The eyed trebles are attached direct on to the split ring, but the uneyed and the swivel are joined by short intermediate lengths of doubled gut or wire, which is secured and bound in the usual way.

Type B is made from three uneyed trebles, a swivel, and two short lengths of gut. The tail hook is bound in first and the other length of gut is fastened by a half-hitch to the eye of the swivel. The other trebles are then bound to the free ends of gut. Twisted gut is very suitable for this purpose.

Sometimes the shanks of the body hooks show an inclination to drop into the slots of the minnow. This can be prevented by placing beads in the positions shown in 100B.

VI

FLOATS

HOME-MADE floats can be built from quills, cork, or paper. There are endless patterns in everyday use, each designed to suit certain conditions of water or different methods of fishing. Thus we have floats for fast water capable of carrying heavy baits and shot ; tiny toothpick floats for fishing lakes and pools ; enormous buoyant floats to indicate the run of a pike ; and heavy sliding floats for fishing the depths of the sea.

We venture to suggest that in the following pages the tackle maker will find instructions for making floats to suit his every need. On the question of choice of pattern we can offer very little advice ; in this connection the angler must be guided by his own knowledge of the water he is about to fish. Failing this, a few local enquiries will no doubt produce the necessary information. It is almost unnecessary to add that floats should at all times be as invisible as possible to the fish, but easily perceptible to the angler. They should be moderately buoyant but not to such an extent as to offer noticeable resistance to the fish which takes the bait. Above all, as in every accessory of angling, they should " balance "—they should be in harmony with the rest of the outfit.

To simplify matters we have classified the floats into three main groups according to the materials used in their construction.

Floats made with Quills

The river angler will find almost everything to meet his needs in this section, a notable exception being the pike float.

Quills fall into five main kinds—the tiny crow quill, beloved of the angler of quiet waters ; the porcupine quill,

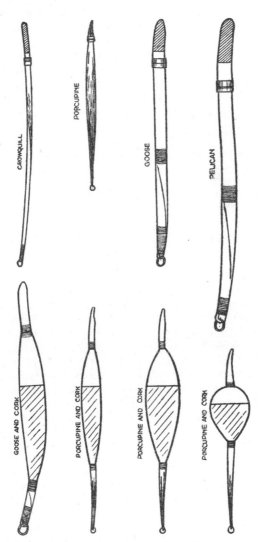

FIG. 101. FLOATS MADE WITH QUILLS

slightly larger but very neat and efficient ; the goose quill, a float which will carry more shot ; and lastly, for heavy work, the pelican and swan quills.

The treatment of the bird quills is the same in every case. Strip off the feathers and generally clean up the quill. It will be noticed that the first few inches of the butt are hollow, but above, a kind of pith is found. In the pithy region, and at a suitable distance from the butt,

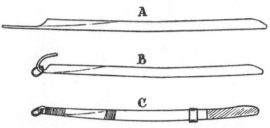

FIG. 102.   MAKING A QUILL FLOAT

cut away the quill in the shape shown in Fig. 102A. This cut, for which a razor blade is used, is made on the inside of the feather's natural curve so that the short extension which is left is of the hard, horny material which runs along the outside.

Slip a small brass wire ring over the strip and fold the latter back as in Fig. 102B. Bind it tightly to the main length, thus securing the ring. Whip again at the weak spot where the hollow tip joins the pithy part. Varnish these two whippings with celluloid varnish and paint the tip of the float in red or white according to choice. When this is dry, varnish the whole lot. This completes the job except for the cap, which is best made from rubber tubing.

A different style of loop mounting is necessary on the porcupine quill and can be used if desired on the others, though it is more particularly suitable for the smaller sizes.

Bend an inch of gauge 24 brass wire into the shape shown in Fig. 103A. This fits on to the bottom end of the quill which may require a little trimming to accommodate it. However, as soon as a snug fit is obtained, bind the wire into position and varnish as before. The result is a very neat and secure fitting.

     *   *   *   *   *

All the quill floats can be made with cork bodies. These give greater buoyancy, thus increasing their capacity for carrying shot—a useful feature in heavy water. Popular

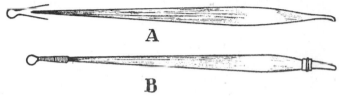

FIG. 103. PORCUPINE QUILL

patterns are a long, thin, tapering body ; a body resembling a slightly elongated egg ; and a dumpy, apple shaped body. All these are shown in Fig. 101.

The first shape, which is usually fitted to goose or porcupine quills, can be made from ordinary medicine bottle corks. The number required depends on the length of the quill, but the finished body should be almost two-thirds of the total length of the float, leaving a slightly greater length of quill exposed at the bottom than at the top.

Bore a hole through the corks. This should be very slightly less than the diameter of the quill. It can be cut with a small rod ferrule sharpened at one end. When the holes are made, push the corks on to the quill and glue each in position pressed tightly against its neighbour.

The uneven shape shown in Fig. 104A is now trimmed down with a razor blade until it looks like the following sketch, after which it is finished with smooth sandpaper.

The top and bottom ends of the cork, being very thin, are liable to break or crumble. To prevent this, bind with silk for a quarter of an inch.

Add the small wire loop at the end and paint the float in any desired colour, after which, varnish the lot.

For the larger sizes—the swan and goose quills—the same method is used for mounting the corks, but a modification can be made, if desired, in the wire loops, so that the float becomes the sliding variety used for fishing deep water.

The principle is shown in Fig. 105 and consists of forming two eyes from some gauge 24 brass wire.   Bind these in

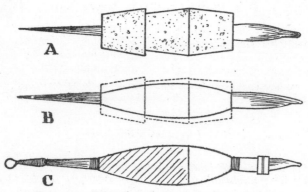

FIG. 104.   PORCUPINE QUILL WITH CORK BODY

position as indicated on the inside of the float's curve, thus giving plenty of running clearance for the line.

The fatter-bodied floats are made in the same way as those already described except that small bung corks take

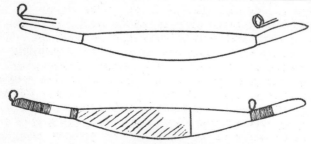

FIG. 105.   NOTTINGHAM SLIDER

the place of medicine bottle corks.   These are cut and sandpapered to any shape the angler may prefer.   Fig. 101 shows a few of the popular types.

Floats made with Cork

Under the previous heading a few floats were mentioned which embodied cork in their construction. The present section deals with cork floats built on wooden centres, much heavier than those built on quill, and used mainly for pike or sea-fishing.

Many anglers use meat-skewers as a centre upon which to build their floats, but these are a trifle too thick to make a neat job. A better plan is to purchase some wood of $\frac{3}{16}$ inch diam. already turned up to shape. A brass ferrule of the same diameter is a very useful tool when the corks have to be drilled. As mentioned before, this is sharpened at one end and makes an excellent borer.

To make floats A, B. and D in Fig. 106, proceed in a similar manner to that already described for cork-bodied quill floats. Cut the wood to length, which may be anything from three to seven inches, and then bore holes in the corks. The diameter of these corks is decided by the type of float. The mackerel pattern may be half or three-quarters of an inch across ; the bass pattern may be anything up to an inch and a half, while the tubby pike float varies from an inch up to two inches.

Choose corks slightly greater than the finished thickness to allow for dressing down. When these are bored, slide them on to the wood and glue them together, pressing tight so that no gaps occur. This stage is equivalent to that shown in Fig. 104A.

Let the glue set, then take the razor blade and trim the corks as near as possible to the desired shape. Follow this by a rub down with a medium file and finish with smooth sandpaper. If any little cracks or faults can be seen in the cork they should be filled with white lead, putty, or plastic wood.

Make the customary small whipping above and below the corks and tie in the bottom loop, which is made from a piece of gauge 20 brass wire bent into the shape shown. The neatness with which this loop is fitted is greatly enhanced by slightly tapering the wood to accommodate it.

After this the float is painted and varnished.

A and B are running floats, so the top eye or loop must

be fitted in the position shown. A screw eye is quite suitable for this purpose providing that the eye part is not too big. See that this is fitted on the same side of the float as the lower eye.

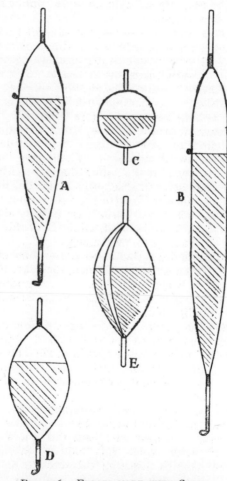

FIG. 106. FLOATS MADE WITH CORK

A = Bass or pollack.   B = Mackerel.   C = Pilot or grayling.
D = Pike float (old style).   E = Pike float.

D can be made as a running or fixed float, according to taste, by adding a screw eye or a cap. It is a pattern which is not very popular today as it has been replaced by the type shown in E.

In making the latter a single piece of cork is preferable. The angler who intends to make a few pike floats should pay a visit to a cork-cutter and get him to turn out a few blanks.

In this pattern the hole is made slightly larger and the wood must correspond. A quarter of an inch is ideal. Bore the hole and push the wood home but do not glue. Trim to the shape shown, by using a razor blade, a file and sandpaper. When this is done take a sharp, thin-bladed knife and cut a vertical V shaped incision from top to bottom of the cork and running right to the centre hole. Then the float can be painted.

The result is the familiar quick-detachable pike float. To fix on the line the wooden centre is withdrawn and the line is inserted via the V shaped incision, its ultimate position in the centre hole being opposite to the slit through which it enters. The wood is then replaced and locks the line in place.

A refinement is sometimes added by sliding a split goose quill inside the hole which acts as a bush in which the line and wooden centre lie.

Fig. 106c is a shape which can be used either as a pilot float for pike or, in the smaller sizes, as a grayling float. It is a single piece of cork bored with a $\frac{3}{16}$ inch hole and shaped into a perfect sphere. As in the last-mentioned pattern, the centre is not glued but is left detachable to effect line adjustments.

* * * * *

Before leaving the question of cork floats let us consider the colour schemes.

First the top—the part which must always be readily visible to the angler. Red, white, and black are colours which each take their turn in supremacy according to conditions of light. The " prepared " angler will always carry a few of each shade.

But the lower half is much more important, since this

is the part which comes within the fish's range of vision. To make an invisible float is beyond the power of any man, as all substantial solid materials are visible. Transparency is a very good substitute for invisibility, but even this has its drawbacks, chief among which is the fact that if the fish does perchance catch a glimpse of it he recognises it as something " foreign."

We consider it far better for a float to be visible and of natural appearance than to be only semi-visible but " foreign " looking. After a series of experiments we have decided that dark brown is by far the best colour. This closely resembles the shade of small natural objects which float along the surface of every river and which cause the fish no alarm. Twigs, dead leaves and alder cones are the chief flotsam on our streams and to these a brown float is sufficiently similar to pass unnoticed. Black, and the hideous greens and blues in common use are so unnatural as to cause suspicion.

Floats made with Paper

Paper floats are very popular among coarse fishermen. This is not to be wondered at for they are light, buoyant, and responsive to the lightest touch.

A long, narrow triangle of paper forms the body. Its base varies in length from 2 to 6 inches and its apex is between 2 feet and 2 feet 6 inches from the base (Fig. 107A).

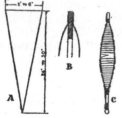

Starting at the base line roll this tightly on to a thin round rod—anything from a knitting needle to a thin pencil, according to the size of the float—until the apex is reached. Apply a dab of Seccotine to the point and so secure it in position. The result is reminiscent of a thin cigar.

FIG. 107.   PAPER FLOAT

When the Seccotine is set, withdraw the object on which the paper has been wound and proceed to make two wooden bungs to seal up the ends (B). These should be just a close fit inside the centre tube. Glue them and insert them to a depth of almost half an inch. The bottom one should be elegantly tapered and finished with the small wire eye as recommended for porcupine quill floats.

At this stage we have found it an advantage to lightly rub down the float with fine sandpaper to remove the "stepped" effect caused by each successive layer of paper. All that remains is painting and varnishing, and the fitting of a soft rubber cap.

Various tapers and body shapes can be produced by slight variations in the shape of the original triangle of paper. In addition to the cigar-shape already described the three patterns shown in Fig. 108 can be made from the appropriate shapes of paper.

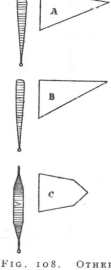

FIG. 108. OTHER PATTERNS OF PAPER FLOATS

Antenna Floats

There is nothing exceptional in the making of these floats. Their chief characteristic is the little projection from the head which enables them to be shotted so that the float itself is submerged. This renders them sensitive to the lightest of bites, for which reason they are especially favoured by roach fishermen.

The projection is actually an extension of the body-centre which may be a thin slip of cane or a tiny crow quill. The whole point is that this should extend above the body and be at least half as long as the total length of the float. The body can be of cork or paper made on the same lines as previous patterns.

If cane is used as a centre the result will look something like Fig. 109A. The core is just a splinter taken from an ordinary garden cane and made round and smooth before building the body thereon. The tip is coloured in bands of red and white to give maximum visibility.

Pattern B has a core of crow quill. The usual method (i.e., having the butt of the quill at the head of the float) is reversed. Instead the butt is at the bottom to form a stem for the attachment of the wire loop.

A good plan is to leave a few whisks of feather at the tip so that the float will be more clearly seen.

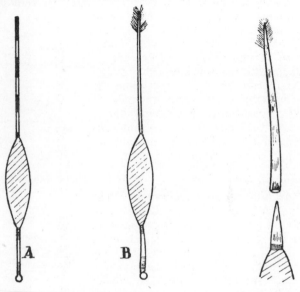

FIG. 109.   ANTENNA FLOATS

FIG. 110.   CON-
VERTIBLE ANTENNA
FLOAT

Almost any pattern of thin quill float can be converted to the Antenna type by capping it with a quill from which the closed end has been cut away (Fig. 110).

VII

CASTS AND TRACES

THE angler who buys shop-made casts is making a great mistake ; there is no item in his equipment which is simple to make, yet it is a job which should be trusted to no other fingers than his own. Whether his cast be made of natural gut, gut-substitute, or wire, it should be made with the meticulous care of the user rather than by the hurried, piece-work movements of the professional.

This applies to all other tackles as well, but to the cast particularly. It must of necessity be of as fine a material as possible, due to the fact that it comes within the fish's range of vision. It is therefore one of the weakest points in the whole outfit, and if it is further weakened by any carelessness in construction it becomes a very vulnerable point which may result in the loss of a fish.

So far as gut or gut-substitute is concerned, it is a proved fact that the weakest points are the knots. These then are the places to watch, and no effort should be spared in making each one perfect. On some tackles it is possible to reduce knot-tying to a minimum, and a few words on this subject are given towards the end of the present chapter.

Casts of Natural Gut

Natural silkworm gut is obtainable in a wide variety of thicknesses ranging from five thousandths of an inch up to twenty-two thousandths. It is therefore suitable for the match fisherman or the salmon angler, and is undoubtedly the best cast material for either.

The trade descriptions of the various grades are very confusing to the uninitiated for they convey no hint as to the thickness or strength of the gut. To simplify this position the following table is given. In it the reader will find the trade name for each grade, its thickness and breaking strain.

This in itself should be a sufficient guide to him in the

L

choice of gut for the making of all level casts, but in case there be any doubt in his mind as to what to use we append other tables which offer suggestions of suitable grades for various fish. For simplicity's sake these are divided under the headings of " level " and " tapered " casts.

Now to the making of the casts.

The first step, which must not on any account be hurried or neglected, is the correct soaking of the gut. The thicker grades should be left in soak for several hours, and the others for at least an hour. Cold water is the best soaking medium, and care must be taken to see that the strands are completely covered. The gut should be withdrawn one strand at a time, as required for knotting, for it dries very quickly after removal from the water.

These strands vary in length from ten to eighteen inches, and a certain amount is cut to waste in the making of each knot. This wastage will be kept as low as possible when proficiency in knotting is attained, but on no account should the thrifty angler tie too closely to the weak " tails " at the end of each strand.

The length of the finished cast is a matter of taste. It varies from the " yard bottom " of the coarse-fisher to the three yard cast of the fly-fisher. The intermediate stages increase in length by steps of half a yard. Colours of gut are usually natural white, blue, peat-brown and green.

Only the necessary number of strands should be put into soak. Water, or even damp, has a very bad effect and any unnecessary wetting should be avoided. Likewise gut should be stored in a dry room, preferably between folds of chamois leather. If kept for long periods the leather should be soaked in glycerine.

If tapered casts are being made, see that the taper is gradual and even, from the thick end to the thin end. No intermediate grade of gut should be omitted. If a cast tapering from 2/5 to 7/5 is being made, the intermediate strengths, 3/5, 4/5, 5/5 and 6/5, should *each* be included in proportions to suit the user.

Cast-making consists mainly of knot-tying, and as the latter subject is one which is very important to the angler, it has been given a chapter to itself. The contents of the present chapter are intended to guide the reader in the selection and treatment of his materials; for the rest he is referred to the chapter on knots. In it he will find all those knots which he is likely to use in cast making; knots for joining and looping gut; knots for attaching gut to swivels for spinning casts; knots for joining droppers to wet-fly casts; and all the knots for attaching the cast to line, hook or fly.

TABLE OF THICKNESSES AND BREAKING STRAINS OF NATURAL GUT

Description.	Thickness in thousandths of an inch.	Breaking Strain.
0/5 undrawn	22	32 lbs.
1/5 ,, ...	21	24 ,,
2/5 ,, ...	20	19 ,,
3/5 ,, ...	19	$15\frac{1}{2}$,,
4/5 ,, ...	18	$12\frac{1}{4}$,,
5/5 ,, ...	17	$10\frac{1}{2}$,,
6/5 ,, ...	16	$8\frac{3}{4}$,,
7/5 ,, ...	15	7 ,,
8/5 ,, ...	14	$4\frac{3}{8}$,,
9/5 ,, ...	13	$3\frac{1}{2}$,,
$\frac{1}{4}$ x drawn	12	$3\frac{1}{8}$,,
$\frac{1}{2}$ x ,, ...	11	$2\frac{7}{8}$,,
$\frac{3}{4}$ x ,, ...	10	$2\frac{1}{2}$,,
1 x ,, ...	9	$2\frac{1}{4}$,,
2 x ,, ...	8	$1\frac{7}{8}$,,
3 x ,, ...	7	$1\frac{5}{8}$,,
4 x ,, ...	$6\frac{1}{2}$	$1\frac{1}{8}$,,
5 x ,, ...	6	13 ozs.
6 x ,, ...	$5\frac{1}{2}$	10 ,,
7 x ,, ...	5	6 ,,

The above breaking strains are based on the gut being dry. Wet gut is a little weaker than dry gut. In the absence of any universal agreement between the tackle makers the trade description given in the left-hand column is subject to slight variations; though, in the main, the above scale is the one in most general use. To avoid misunderstanding when ordering it is advisable to state the thickness in thousandths of an inch.

TABLE OF RECOMMENDED GUT SIZES FOR LEVEL CASTS

NOTE.—The first mentioned figure represents the thicker grade of gut.

Extra heavy salmon or sea fishing - - -	0/5 or 1/5
Medium salmon, bass or pollack - - -	2/5 or 3/5
Small salmon or bass in clear water -	4/5 or 5/5
Grilse, small bass, or barbel, etc. - - -	6/5 or 7/5
Large trout, tench, perch, chub, bream, etc. -	7/5 to 9/5
As above but for finer fishing - - - -	$\frac{1}{4}$ x to 1 x
Fine roach, dace, trout, etc. - - - -	2 x or 3 x
Extra fine - - - - - - -	4 x or 5 x
Match fishing - - - - - -	4 x to 7 x

It is impossible to give a recommendation for every type of British fish, but the above table will be found to cover a representative variety. The reader can thus work out the correct grade for any fish which is not mentioned.

e.g For heavy carp use the same grade as for barbel ; for grayling the same as for fine trout, etc.

TABLE OF RECOMMENDED GUT SIZES FOR TAPERED CASTS

Salmon—stout - - - -	- 0/5 tapering to	3/5
,, —medium - - -	- 0/5 ,,	,, 4/5
,, —fine - - - -	- 2/5 ,,	,, 5/5
,, —extra fine - - -	- 2/5 ,,	,, 6/5
Sea-trout and Grilse—stout -	- 1/5 ,,	,, 4/5
,, ,, —medium -	- 2/5 ,,	,, 6/5
,, ,, —fine - -	- 2/5 ,,	,, 7/5
,, ,, —extra fine -	- 3/5 ,,	,, 8/5
Trout—stout - - - -	- 6/5 ,,	,, 9/5
,, —medium - - - -	- 8/5 ,,	,, $\frac{1}{2}$ x
,, —fine - - - -	- $\frac{1}{4}$ x ,,	,, 1 x
,, —extra fine - - -	- $\frac{1}{2}$ x ,,	,, 4 x

The above recommendations are subject to wide variations to suit varying conditions. Some anglers use casts of rapid and considerable taper ; others prefer those of very little taper. This table will serve as a guide to the beginner in his first attempt at cast-making, but when he is more conversant with the various strengths and tapers he will no doubt indulge his own fancy. In this connection he will probably find that the table of strengths on a previous page will give him some guidance.

Note.—The above recommendations do not include twisted gut. This is frequently used in the thicker end of tapered salmon casts of high breaking strain. Where used it should be carefully graded to blend with the following strands of single gut, otherwise a kinked cast will occur.

Casts of Gut Substitute.

Unfortunately it is impossible to give the same statistics for gut-substitute as have been given for silk-worm gut. This is because each manufacturer seems to adopt a different key-scale in the marketing of his product.

We realize, however, that a little guidance is necessary in the selection of material and so have prepared the scale given herewith. In it is given the thickness in thousandths of an inch, the approximate breaking strains of good qualities, and the size designation of *natural* gut of the same *thickness*. This last is intended to give the user some idea of the *appearance* of the substitute if he is already conversant with the thicknesses of natural gut. It is no guide to the *strength* as there is a wide disparity in the breaking strains of natural and substitute of the same thickness.

The given breaking strains should be quite sufficient to guide the angler in his selection.

This material can be obtained in lengths of 5, 40 and 100 yards. A considerable saving is effected by purchasing the greater lengths. Compared with natural gut it has the advantage of being devoid of knots, but is less translucent and deteriorates more rapidly in water.

Soaking must take place as usual before any knots are tied. For these the reader is once again referred to the chapter on the subject; there is one additional note, however. Gut-substitute knots or loops are more inclined to slip than those of natural gut. This is not by any means a frequent occurrence, but, should the angler so desire, he can reduce to a minimum the possibilities of such a happening by whipping in the short end of gut which would normally be cut away.

TABLE OF THICKNESSES AND BREAKING-STRAINS OF GUT-SUBSTITUTE

Thickness in thousandths of an inch.				Approximate Breaking Strain.		Equivalent Thickness of Natural Gut.
6	..	..	..	..	5 ozs.	5 x drawn
7	..	..	..	..	11 ,,	3 x ,,
8	..	..	..	..	$2\frac{1}{2}$ lbs.	2 x ,,
9	..	..	..	..	$5\frac{1}{2}$,,	1 x ,,
10	..	..	..	..	$8\frac{1}{4}$,,	$\frac{3}{4}$ x ,,
12	..	..	..	..	$9\frac{3}{4}$,,	$\frac{1}{4}$ x ,,
14	..	..	..	..	$11\frac{3}{4}$,,	8/5 undrawn
16	..	..	..	..	$13\frac{3}{4}$,,	6/5 ,,
18	..	..	..	..	$16\frac{1}{4}$,,	4/5 ,,
20	..	..	..	..	$18\frac{3}{4}$,,	2/5 ,,
22	..	..	..	..	$20\frac{1}{2}$,,	0/5 ,,
24	..	..	..	..	23 ,,	Not made
26	..	..	..	..	25 ,,	,,
28	..	..	..	..	$27\frac{1}{2}$,,	,,
30	..	..	..	..	$30\frac{3}{4}$,,	,,
32	..	..	..	..	33 ,,	,,
34	..	..	..	..	38 ,,	,,
36	..	..	..	..	46 ,,	,,
38	..	..	..	..	54 ,,	,,
40	..	..	..	..	65 ,,	,,
45	..	..	..	..	78 ,,	,,
50	..	..	..	..	85 ,,	,,

The breaking strains given apply only to the best qualities. Inferior grades are of very uncertain strengths.

Avoiding Knots.

It has been previously mentioned that the knot is the weakest point in the cast. This is even more true of gut substitute than of natural gut. Certain knots cannot be avoided, but there are others which can be replaced by a suitable binding. Gut substitute lends itself much more readily than gut to this process ; in fact, it can be carried out to such an extent that there is scarcely a vulnerable knot in the whole cast.

In Fig. 111A, a simple method of forming a loop without knotting is shown. True, there is a half hitch in the short

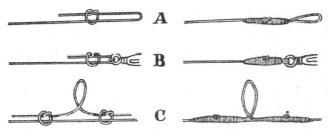

FIG. 111. AVOIDING KNOTS IN MAIN LENGTHS OF
GUT SUBSTITUTE

end of gut, but as this is not subjected to any direct strain it is not nearly so likely to break as would a loop formed by, say, a figure-of-eight knot.

The half hitch knot in the short length of gut is knotted around the main length. Each is then bound to the other by means of strong, well-waxed silk ; after which the binding is varnished with celluloid or shellac.

It may appear that a loop thus formed is liable to pull out. If the job is properly done, however, the loop will not part under a strain which would be sufficient to break a knotted cast. In other words, the knot is weaker than the binding.

The same remarks apply to B and C. The former is a method of securing gut or gut-substitute to the eye of a swivel, as when making a spinning trace. The latter is more useful to sea fishermen for eliminating the intermediate loop knots on gut paternosters.

Traces made of Wire.

These heavier traces are usually used for spinning for large fish such as pike and salmon, and when spinning or bottom-fishing for the bigger varieties of sea fish.

Wire can be purchased in a variety of grades ranging from a fine single strand which is almost as invisible as gut,

up to heavy Bowden cable. The leading tackle manufacturers sell a rustless, cable-laid, steel wire which they
produce in various thicknesses. This is ideal except for
the finest work, where a single strand is preferable.

Probably the smallest and finest of wire traces is that
used for thread-line spinning for salmon or pike. It may
seem strange to use anything so heavy as wire with a fixed-
spool reel, but there is a need of something strong enough
to resist the effects of contact with the teeth of the fish.
However, to conform to the principles of thread-line
spinning the wire should be as fine as possible.

The length of these casts seldom exceeds eighteen inches.
A hook swivel is secured to one end for attaching to the
lure. To the other end an ordinary small swivel is attached
which in turn is tied to the line.

With single wire the swivels can be made perfectly secure
by simply twisting the wire as in Fig. 112. It is inserted

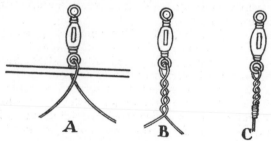

A   B   C

FIG. 112. HOW TO MOUNT A SWIVEL ON WIRE

through the eye of the swivel and bent over, but before
starting to twist, a knitting needle is inserted as shown in
Fig. 112A. This preserves a small loop and prevents the
wire from closing too tightly on to the swivel. The two
wires are then twisted *each around the other* for several turns,
following which the shorter end is coiled tightly around the
main length. The separate processes can be easily dis-
tinguished from the sketch.

For heavier spinning it is usual to employ a cast of
between three feet and six feet long. These should be
divided into three or four equal parts and re-united by

swivels. The same system of attachment (Fig. 112) can be used, but if the trace is made of multi-strand twisted wire, it would be advisable to run a little solder over the coils after securing the swivels.

Swivels on spinning casts should always be as small as possible. A small swivel will stand a considerable strain and is much less alarming to the fish. They should be tested before fitting, to see that they work properly and are free from rust. A faulty swivel will result either in a dragging bait or a kinked line.

For tope or heavy sea fishing the trace should be of very strong wire, at least six feet long, and incorporating three or four swivels of proportionate strength. If twisted wire is used the swivels should be secured as in Fig. 97A and B, after which the short end should be bound to the main length with thin copper wire, and finally secured with solder.

Fig. 97c shows how single-strand rustless steel wire is attached. If this is used, it should be of gauge 20.

When casts are made up, they should be smeared with vaseline and kept in greaseproof envelopes. Rust, particularly in the finer gauges, will perhaps result in a lost fish.

VIII

WIREWORK

THIS chapter is mainly for the sea-angler. It deals with those uses of wire which have not been described under previous headings ; it concerns the various types of booms, paternosters, and lead links which are indispensable for sea-fishing.

But it is not exclusively for the sea-angler. The principles of general elementary wirework are here given, to which frequent references are made in other chapters ; and details of tools and equipment are to be found in the opening section.

It is, therefore, advisable that the reader who intends making *any* tackles which incorporate wire in their design, should first study the following instructions.

The Equipment.

The tackle maker who intends doing regular wirework will first need to purchase two pairs of suitable pliers. To have the right tools for the job will considerably lessen the labour, and will add immensely to the efficiency of the finished product.

The two recommended types are illustrated in Fig. 113. On the left we have the kind with the round tapering jaws. These are used for the formation of all loops and bends. The rounded jaws form a pattern on which the wire is worked. They are so useful as to be almost indispensable.

The other type is used solely for cutting, but for this purpose they are superior to any other, in that they will cut much closer and can be used in positions where other varieties would be unsatisfactory.

A third useful type—which it is unnecessary to illustrate —is the ordinary standard pattern as used by mechanics and electricians. They are mainly used for gripping while the wire is being bent or cut with the types previously mentioned.

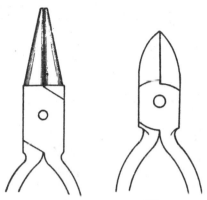

FIG. 113. PLIERS USED IN WIREWORK

The last variety can be bought from any sixpenny stores, but we strongly advise that the other two should be of as good a quality as the angler can afford. Cheap tools soon give notice and result in unsatisfactory work.

As regards the wire itself the most popular and effective is brass, in gauges 17, 18, 19 and 20. If possible it should be oxydized or bronzed to reduce its visibility to the fish. Do not worry too much about this, however, as an hour in salt water will remove its pristine shininess.

An alternative to brass is rustless steel which has many good points and some bad. Its chief advantage is that it is very strong and is absolutely impervious to the action of brine, whereas brass is liable to become brittle. Against this however we have several objections. First it is harder to work because of its greater strength ; it is very bright and may cause alarm to the fish ; it is also much more expensive. We consider that these last two objections are sufficient to turn the scales in favour of brass, at least, so far as the tackles described in the following chapter are concerned. On certain other tackles mentioned in this book rustless steel wire is preferable to brass. Where this is the case it is specified in the text.

Booms

Dozens of varieties of tackles are made from wire but nearly all of them embody the simple loop or eye for the attachment of line or cast.   Perhaps, then, we should begin by explaining how this is formed.   In a plain boom it is used thrice so we will make this our first example.

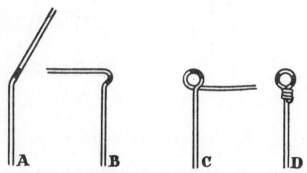

FIG. 114. THE FORMATION OF A WIRE LOOP

(The dark marks show the position of the jaws of the pliers.)

Take a piece of wire (gauge 19 or 20) of 12 inches long. Two inches from one end grip with the round-jawed pliers and bend as shown (Fig. 114A).   This bend should be only very slight or a lop-sided loop will result.   Keeping the pliers in the same position and using the fingers of the left hand, bring the wire over the round jaw until it looks something like B.   The grip of the pliers is now changed.   Instead of gripping in the original bend we take hold at the point which will ultimately become the top of our loop.   This change will help us in the next step.   Still working with the left hand pull the wire-end down and round until it has formed a complete circle and is lying at right angles to the main length (c).   Again the grip is changed.   This time the loop lies flat between the jaws.   The end of wire is brought round the main stem for three close turns and any surplus is cut away with the cutting pliers (D).

It is important to get the correct grip at each stage.   To clarify this point the wire in the illustrations has been darkened at those points which lie between the jaws of the pliers as each bend is accomplished.

At a distance of $1\frac{1}{2}$ inches from our first loop we proceed to make another, this time working with the long free end of the wire in the left hand while the pliers are held, as usual, in the right. When this loop is made we do not cut away the surplus wire as this now becomes the main arm of the boom. Having secured the second loop with three turns as before we carry the remaining length of wire at right angles to the short stem already formed. At its free end we make

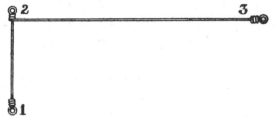

FIG. 115. A PLAIN BOOM

a third and final loop exactly the same as our first, and our boom is complete (Fig. 115). In the illustration the loops are numbered in accordance with the order in which they are made.

This is the simplest form of boom but is a most satisfactory pattern. The line is passed through loop 2, twisted three or four times round the short shank and brought out at loop 1. The lead is attached to this loose end of line and the cast is passed over and through loop 3.

*　　　*　　　*　　　*　　　*

Some anglers demand a more elaborate boom complete with swivels and lead link. This can be made by placing a swivel on loop 1 before the final twists are formed. To the other eye of the swivel the lead link is attached. The latter is started by making the usual loop, which in this case must be affixed to the bottom eye of the swivel before sealing. Three inches below, bend the wire at right angles; two inches further bend upwards at right angles; and finally at a point one inch higher up double the wire back over this last inch and cut away the surplus. The result is illustrated in Fig. 116A.   With the fingers the lead link is

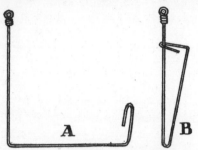

FIG. 116.   MAKING A LEAD LINK

now bent to its working position (Fig. 116B).   Fig. 117

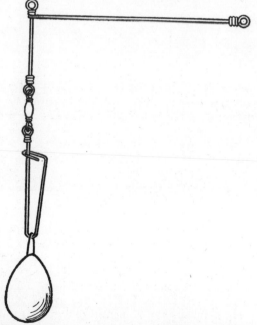

FIG. 117.   BOOM AND LEAD LINK UNITED BY SWIVEL

shows the completed job duly mounted on the boom and
with the lead in position.

A simpler boom and lead link can be made by omitting the swivel. The finished job consists of a single piece of wire and is shown in Fig. 118. In view of the previous

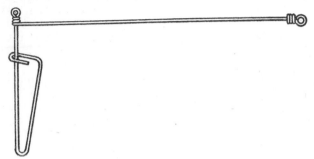

FIG. 118. BOOM AND LEAD LINK IN ONE

explanation it is a simple matter to construct this by reference to the sketch.

Paternosters

The paternoster is a tackle embodying two or three booms which are interconnected by wire or gut substitute. The latter is preferable as it can be obtained in very strong grades and is less visible and more flexible than wire. A simple and effective pattern can be made as follows.

Bend three pieces of wire (gauge 18 or 19) to the shape

FIG. 119. BOOM AS USED ON PATERNOSTER

shown in Fig. 119. Take four feet of extra strong gut substitute and after soaking well in cold water, make a loop at each end (See chapter on knots). These loops should be about 1¼ inch long. Next tie three simple half hitch knots in the main length of the gut ; the first, three inches from one end ; the next fifteen inches above, and the last a further fifteen inches above the second. This last end is to be the top end of our paternoster (Fig. 120).

To facilitate the handling of the gut during the following stages it is a good plan to hang it from a hook by the top loop. A further advantage is to fit a small sea lead to the bottom loop. This will keep the gut taut.

Lay the short arm of one of the booms against the gut, pointing in a downwards direction. The bottom half hitch knot should be opposite the middle point of the short arm (Fig. 120A). Now whip the wire to the gut with strong well-waxed thread. Start the whipping close into the angle of the boom and continue down, missing the knot, until the end of the short arm is reached.

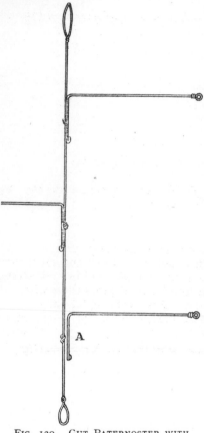

FIG. 120. GUT PATERNOSTER WITH WIRE BOOMS

The next boom is fitted in exactly the same manner but faces away from the gut in the opposite direction to the bottom one. The top boom faces the same way as the bottom boom. The illustration (Fig. 120) shows the general appearance of the tackle, including the knots and loops. These knots are to prevent the binding from slipping, but additional security can be obtained by enclosing the short arm of the boom within the half-hitch and following up with a binding as before.

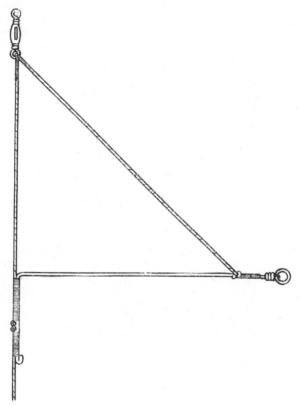

FIG. 121. EXTRA SUPPORT FOR THE BOOM

When every boom is fixed, the binding should be varnished as a protection against rotting. To complete the paternoster a swivel is passed through the top loop, and a lead link through the bottom.

There are many variations of this pattern. A reinforced edition is shown in Fig. 121. On this type the main gut is

M

in three short lengths, each connected with a swivel.   From each swivel to the end of the boom immediately below it, a short length of gut substitute is bound or knotted into position as shown in Fig 121.   The methods of attaching

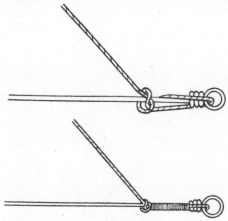

FIG. 122.   ATTACHING GUT TO BOOM

gut to swivels and boom are shown in Figs 122 and 123. This extra piece of gut gives a straight pull on any fish

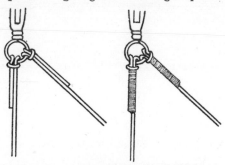

FIG. 123.   ATTACHING GUT TO SWIVEL

which is hooked.   In this respect it is an advantage but it has the disadvantage of adding to the general bulk of the tackle ; a paternoster is one of the worst offenders in this respect.

Another variation with good and bad points is the gut-substitute loop for hook attachment. This replaces the wire loop at the end of the boom. Knot the gut-sub. as in Fig. 124A, then bend the end of the wire in the manner shown (B). Now lay the two together, whip and varnish (C). The result is a very nice hook loop but one which may eventually become frayed or rotten. However, when this happens it can be removed

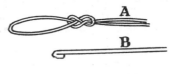

FIG. 124.   GUT LOOPS FOR
PATERNOSTER

and replaced. This same loop can also be used on the single boom tackle if desired.

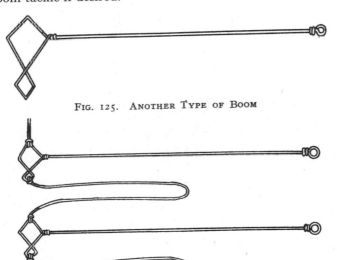

FIG. 125.   ANOTHER TYPE OF BOOM

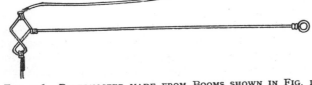

FIG. 126.   PATERNOSTER MADE FROM BOOMS SHOWN IN FIG. 125

Another simple form of paternoster can be made by bending the booms as shown in Fig. 125. These are united by short lengths of gut substitute looped at each end, with an extra piece at top and bottom to hold the swivel and lead link respectively (Fig. 126). Gauge 18 wire is used.

*   *   *   *   *

The type of lead link hitherto mentioned is simple to make but is not the most reliable in use. A more dependable pattern can be made as follows.

Take a piece of gauge 18 wire about eight inches in length and bend it into the shape of an elongated letter U. The distance between the parallel sides should not exceed ⅜ths

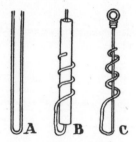

FIG. 127.   A VERY SECURE LEAD LINK

of an inch (Fig. 127A). Over one of the sides place a small metal tube (an old thin ferrule will do) to act as a mould around which to coil the wire. Proceed to bend as in the illustration (Fig. 127B). When three or four turns have been made the remaining wire of that length can be trimmed away. Now remove the tube and bend a loop on to the end of the centre piece of wire. The finished product is shown in Fig. 127C.

A running boom is another useful tackle that the angler can make at home. For best results a thicker wire, gauge 17, is preferable. The loops or eyes at each end of the boom are different from the types previously described in that they are formed by a double turn. This gives a

smoother inside surface which will not trap the running
line.

Fig. 128 gives an idea of the appearance of the completed

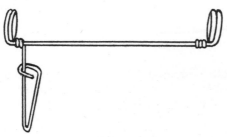

FIG. 128. RUNNING BOOM

tackle from which the angler can easily work out the method
by which it is made.

IX

LEADS AND MOULDS

L EAD making is a very simple business which is seldom carried our properly. Many sea-anglers cast rough leads by pouring the molten metal into a crude mould such as a small tin lid. Others cut sections from lead piping and make a hole through which to pass the wire loop. These leads are extremely rough in finish but are no doubt suitable for the purpose for which they are intended.

There are other anglers however, who are not content to fish with such primitive tackle ; the only answer to their requirements is a properly moulded lead, which they usually purchase from the tackle shop. To cast these at home, a chill or mould is required, and these are rather expensive.

We require a properly moulded home-made lead without the expense of buying a chill. There is but one solution— to first make the chill, after which we can cast leads to our heart's delight.

Many anglers would cast their leads at home if only they had a suitable mould. Very few have undertaken to make one because it seems a difficult job. Actually it can be made for a few pence and is quite simple.

The Mould

First decide on the type of lead to be made—let us say, a four ounce sea lead. Purchase from the tackle shop a lead of the chosen type. This is required for a pattern from which all your home-made leads will be cast.

The next essential is a piece of smooth, perfectly flat wood three inches square and $\frac{3}{4}$ inch thick. The edges and surfaces should be absolutely true.

Lay the lead in the centre of the square and mark carefully the exact outline of its shape, excluding the wire. Now with a gouge carve out a recess in the said shape so that the lead lies in it snugly. This cavity should be of a depth exactly half the thickness of the lead, so that the lead is precisely half above and half below the surface of the wood (Fig. 129).

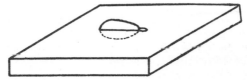

FIG. 129. LEAD RECESSED HALF-WAY IN WOODEN BASE.

Having assured a good fit and an exact depth, the lead can be temporarily removed to facilitate the next part of the programme. This consists of making wooden sides to a depth of ¾ inch all round the square of wood, thus turning it into a little box. This is best done by screwing strips of wood 1½ inch wide to the sides of our original square which,

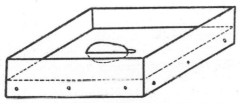

FIG. 130. SIDES SCREWED INTO POSITION

being itself ¾ inch thick, will leave an inside depth of ¾ inch (Fig. 130).

Put the lead inside in its little recess and press firmly into position, taking care that the wire loop lies flat and close to the wood. The exposed half of the lead is now lightly covered with oil to prevent adhesion to the plaster from which the mould is to be made.

Mix up sufficient plaster of Paris to fill the box, and place this in bit by bit so that it is driven into every corner. Be sure that it is well pressed into position around the lead. Fill up the box to the level of its sides and scoop off any surplus by drawing a table knife across the top. Your lead is thus covered beneath ¾ inch of plaster.   This is put away for a few days until thoroughly hardened.

When the angler is satisfied that the plaster is set he can unscrew the side pieces of his box and remove the first half of his mould.

Take a piece of good smooth paper (a thick writing paper will do) and cut from it a 3-inch square, from which in turn the pattern of the lead (excluding wire) should be cut.   Lay the paper on the plaster to see that the shape is correct and that it fits close around the outer edge of the lead. The paper is then soaked in oil.

The purpose of this paper is to act as an insulator between the first half of the plaster cast and the one which we are about to make, otherwise the two halves of the mould would be stuck together with the lead in their middle.

Our next need is a box of 1½ inch *inside* depth and 3 inches square.   This can be made from our original side strips of wood with a new bottom piece fastened outside instead of inside.

In the bottom of our new box we lay the first half of our mould, lead uppermost of course.   The exposed surface of lead is again brushed with oil after which the oiled paper is placed in position.

All is now ready to receive the next supply of plaster which should be placed carefully as before until the box is filled and the surplus removed.   A further three days is allowed for the drying of the mould.

FIG. 131.   THE FIRST HALF OF THE MOULD, SHOWING IMPRESSION OF LEAD, AND DUCT THROUGH WHICH MOLTEN METAL IS POURED

When set, the box can be unscrewed, the mould separated, the lead removed and the paper thrown away.   We now have two blocks of plaster each 3 inches square and ¾ inch thick, both containing a half impression of our lead, but so far we have no duct through which to pour the molten lead when we commence casting.

This can be made by cutting a narrow channel in one half of the mould, from the *bottom* of the lead cavity to the outside. (Fig. 131). It should be slightly flared as illustrated so that the lead pours in easily.

At this stage it is advisable to place the mould in a warm room and leave for at least a fortnight. This is done to allow all moisture to disappear. A slightly damp mould will cause molten lead to spit in a dangerous manner.

Casting the Lead.

When it is all ready for use we place a sufficient quantity of lead in a wrought iron ladle and place it on the fire or over a gas ring ; meanwhile we occupy our time with bending to shape the wire loops by which the lead is attached when fishing. One half of our mould will contain an impression of this loop so we bend our wire to fit. The ends however must be extended and bent into the shape illustrated (Fig. 132), so that they do not pull out when subjected to a strain. One of these loops should be placed in its correct groove in the mould, which can now be put together and held by a strong rubber band. The mouth of the duct should be facing upwards.

FIG. 132.
SHAPE OF
WIRE USED
IN SEA
LEADS

As soon as the lead melts it is poured into the duct. Replace the ladle on the fire to keep the lead hot ; open up your mould and there you have a perfect 4-oz. sea lead which looks as if it might have been cast in an expensive metal mould. Any rough edges can easily be trimmed with a file.

Whatever type of lead is required, providing it is cast and not rolled or stamped, it can be made by the above method. Shape, at least so far as anglers leads are concerned, makes little difference. Moulds can be made for all types and sizes used in sea fishing, spinning etc. The keen tackle maker can save a considerable amount in cash once the moulds are made.

Other Leads

So much for the cast leads. There are other types which

can best be made from sheet lead.   The tackle manufacturers usually stamp these out by machinery but the amateur can make sufficient for his own requirements by the use of scissors The fold-over and· flat anti-kink varieties are the most popular examples of this type.

Sheet lead of various thicknesses can be obtained from plumbers or builder's merchants.   A couple of shillings-worth will make a lot of leads.

The two most commonly used shapes are illustrated in Fig. 133.   These are cut from a small square of the sheet metal—this facilitates handling.

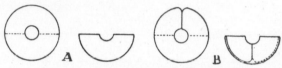

FIG. 133.   FOLD-OVER ANTI-KIᴺK LEADS

In A the square has been trimmed to a circle and the centre is punched out (an old ferrule of suitable thickness sharpened at one end, makes an excellent punch).   The lead is then folded and is ready for use.   This type of lead can be made in all sizes and is most useful in all forms of spinning.

Type B is more complicated though perhaps a little more efficient.   When in use the line or cast crosses over in the middle of the lead from the flap on one side to that on the other.   The risk of loss is thus reduced to a minimum.

The scraps of metal which are cut to waste when making the last-mentioned types, should be saved for the melting-pot.   They will be useful when cast leads are being made.

Practically the only types of lead which cannot be made at home by the above processes are ordinary shot and the small body leads for minnow-spinning.   The former the angler will be obliged to buy unless he uses a substitute such as a small fold-over, but the latter have already been dealt with in the section devoted to the making of spinning tackles.

X

NET-MAKING

THERE are many other uses for nets, apart from those of the angler, so this chapter may be doubly useful to some of its readers.

Net-making proper, as practised by professional fishermen and others, is an extremely interesting subject, though it may perhaps become a little tedious for those who earn their living by it. It is fascinating to watch an expert at work ; to see the speed and deftness of his movements, and the ease with which they are made. Such a practical demonstration will convey to the onlooker a much better idea of the process than can be given in black-and-white but that is usually the case. Nevertheless, it is by no means difficult to learn ; the careful beginner can make almost as good a net as the professional, but it will take him a much longer time to produce. With practice, however, the movements of the fingers become more economical and certain, and it is not long before the novice can work at surprising speed.

Nets are of two main types—the plain unshaped net sometimes used by the professional fisherman, and the shaped nets. Most of the angler's nets belong to the latter section, the only exception being a small-mesh plain net sometimes used when dragging for minnows for bait.

The Equipment

There are only two tools required—a shuttle and a spool. These are illustrated in Fig. 134. The shuttle (A) is of the most popular type, though other patterns are obtainable. They are made of wood, bone, or erinoid, the latter being preferable. The shuttle serves two purposes : it acts as a needle for working in and out of the meshes, and it also carries the twine with which the net is made. It is so designed that it will readily release the necessary amount of twine for each operation. When purchasing the shuttle the angler should persuade the shopkeeper to show him how to fill it, as this idea is almost impossible to convey except by practical demonstration.

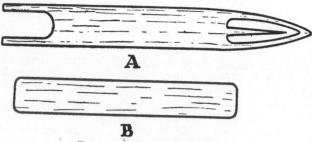

FIG. 134.   NET-MAKING TOOLS
A = Shuttle.   B = Spool.

The spool (B) is just a plain, flat piece of wood, polished smoothly and with sharp corners removed. It is six inches long and of a width to suit the size of mesh required. An old boxwood foot-rule, trimmed to the desired length and width, makes a fine spool.

Both the shuttle and the spool vary in size according to the size of mesh required. The size of the shuttle is of no great importance, providing that it passes freely through the meshes. But the spool is all-important, as it entirely controls the size of the mesh. Its width should be a little less than a quarter of the outside circumference of the mesh—thus a spool of three-eighths of an inch wide will make a mesh of two inches round, or half an inch from knot to knot. Several sizes of spools should be made so that the angler is equipped to deal with any size of mesh. Three shuttles—small, medium and large—will cover all requirements.

Twine should be selected according to the job it has to do. For small meshes a thin, pliable texture is necessary. Thick, harsh twine is only suitable for heavy work and large meshes. "Doped" waterproofed twine is also obtainable, but is generally speaking only necessary for use in salt water.

A Plain Net.

The first item is to make a support on which the first row of meshes is to be made. For this purpose a thin wooden curtain-rod is ideal. It should be fixed at each end in just the same manner as when used for supporting a curtain, but it is preferable to fix it across an open space (such as a doorway) rather than against a wall. A strong cord stretched tightly between two hooks will also serve the purpose, but is not so satisfactory as the rod.

Having filled your shuttle, proceed to make a series of equidistant loops along the rod from left to right, tying each one with a clove-hitch. The length of twine forming each loop must be slightly less than half the outside circumference of the predetermined mesh, to allow for the amount used in tying each clove-hitch. The knot is shown in the first illustration (Fig. 135A), and the second shows the appearance of the first row of loops.

The number of loops is chosen according to the *width* of the net. Upon them it is possible to build any desired length.

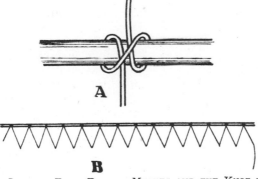

FIG. 135. SHOWING FIRST ROW OF MESHES AND THE KNOT BY WHICH THEY ARE ATTACHED

By working from left to right we have reached the extreme right-hand end of our row of meshes, and we now wish to start on the second row. If we are working in a doorway, as suggested, we simply walk through to the other side, so that we are again working from left to right. It is a great advantage to thus change sides after each row so that we are always working in the same direction. Thus, we are now facing our work with the shuttle at our left ready for the second row of meshes.

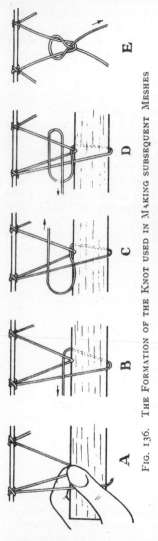

FIG. 136. THE FORMATION OF THE KNOT USED IN MAKING SUBSEQUENT MESHES

Before starting the second row we must learn a new knot—the Sheet Bend. The movements for tying are shown in Fig. 136. The V-shaped loop is the first on the left of our first row of meshes, and the point is held down between the thumb and forefinger of the left hand, while the top edge of the spool is held close against it (Fig. 136A). The positions of the forefinger and thumb are shown in the first illustration, but are omitted from the subsequent ones in order than the knot shall be clearly seen.

Bring the shuttle down across the front of the spool and pass up behind : pass it through the loop from behind ; carry it over to the left until it tightens on the spool ; and trap the whole lot against the spool with the thumb. This is shown, minus the thumb, in Fig. 136B.

Leaving a loose loop (bight) of line lying to the left, bring the shuttle across the front of the V to the right (C). Pass the shuttle behind the V, out through the previously-formed bight (D) and pull tight (E).

The pulling tight of the knot should be done very carefully so that the genuine result (E) is obtained. Careless tightening will cause a faulty knot, which will allow the meshes to slip. Another point to keep in mind is that the twine around the spool should be first drawn fairly tight (as in B) and held securely under the thumb during the rest of the process. It must be remembered that the twine which lies around the spool is the new mesh just being formed. If it is allowed to go slack it will be bigger than the other meshes.

Thus is formed the first mesh of our second row.

Do not remove the spool; it is long enough to carry several meshes and will hold more securely if the finished

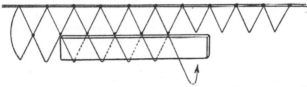

FIG. 137. SHOWING HOW THE MESHES ARE FORMED AROUND THE SPOOL

meshes are left on while we work from left to right (Fig. 137). As soon as it begins to get full it is an easy matter to slide off those meshes on the left.

From where we left off—i.e. the knotting of our last mesh—the process is exactly the same. Take the point of the second loop of the first row and hold it against the spool, between thumb and forefinger as before. From the

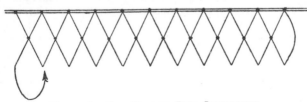

FIG. 138. THE SECOND ROW COMPLETED.

last-made knot bring the twine down across the front of the spool and pass up behind, pass it through the loop and form the knot. Once again across the spool, through the next loop, knot again, and so on to the end of the second row (Fig. 138).

Then we go through the doorway as before and proceed to make the third row of meshes.

The only point where the reader may possibly go wrong is when starting a new row of meshes, but a careful study of Fig. 136B will convey the correct idea, and the last right-hand mesh in Fig. 138 will show what it looks like when finished.

Once the " hang " of the thing is acquired, it is amazing how rapidly the work can be done, even by a raw beginner. The movements as described in the text and illustrations are by far the most economical ; they should be followed implicitly until they become mechanical. Thus a great saving of time will be made.

Once the first row of meshes is formed the reader can continue to lay on the subsequent rows to any desired length.

Shaped Nets.

There is very little more to learn, but this section will enable the reader to apply his knowledge to the making of landing-nets, keep-nets, etc.

One of the simplest ways of making a landing-net is to build it up on a circular frame. For this purpose the frame of the net itself is ideal. As before, we commence by forming a series of loops round the frame, securing each with a clove-hitch. Make the loops at even distances all round the frame until the starting-point is reached. The spare end of the first clove-hitch should then be tied to

FIG. 139.   FIRST AND LAST MESHES (FIRST ROW) OF A CIRCULAR NET

the end of the last mesh by means of a reef-knot (Fig. 139). In the illustration it is impossible to show the whole ring to which the meshes are attached. We have, therefore, shown only the starting and finishing meshes, and the method by which they are united. After tying the ends with a reef knot the twine is cut free before starting on the second row.

Hold your first loop between the forefinger and thumb and tie a sheet-bend as shown in Fig. 140A, but leave a

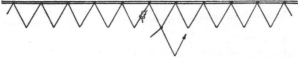

FIG. 140A. STARTING THE SECOND ROW (CIRCULAR NET)

short piece hanging free for tying in the end mesh of the second row. Now bring the spool into use again, and continue making the second row as described in the previous chapter, until the starting point is reached once more. Again unite the last mesh to the first by means of a reef

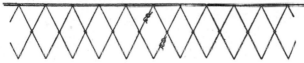

FIG. 140B. FINISH OF SECOND ROW.

knot (Fig. 140B), cut away the twine and commence the third row as before. We are thus working in circles around the net.

When a few meshes have been laid on in this way it is time to start tapering the net. This can be done in either or both of the following ways: by dropping meshes or by decreasing the size of the mesh.

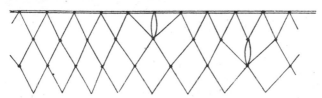

FIG. 141. DROPPING MESHES

The process of dropping meshes is illustrated in Fig. 141. As the shuttle is brought up behind the spool preparatory

N

to passing through the loop, it is passed through two consecutive loops instead of one.   The result, in the next row,
is one less mesh for every one so dropped in the previous
row.   It is usual to drop meshes at regular intervals along
the row.   Thus, for gradual tapers we may drop every
fifth or sixth ; or for more rapid tapers, every second or
third.   If we drop every fifth mesh from a row of forty
meshes there are only thirty-two in the following row.
If from this row we drop every fourth mesh there will be
but twenty-four in the next row.   By this method the net
is tapered, rapidly or gradually as desired, until it reaches
unworkably small proportions.   A piece of twine is then
passed through the remaining loops, and they are tied
together in a bunch.   The net is then complete.

*   *   *   *   *

Another way of obtaining taper is by gradually decreasing
the width of the spool *after each row of meshes is completed*.
This results in a smaller mesh, which causes the net to
decrease in size, but stitches must be dropped as before
when it is time to finish off.

This scheme of decreasing the size of the meshes can be
very well applied to a keep-net.   At the top, or mouth,
a wide spool is used to form the wide meshes.   A rapid
taper forming the " neck " is produced by decreasing the
size of the spool, after which the net widens out again to
the " body " part by using the larger spools once more.

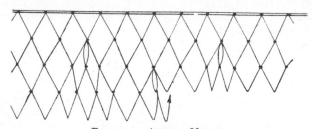

Fig. 142.   Adding Meshes

Another way of increasing the size of the net is by *adding*
meshes.   A small loop is formed between the proper meshes,
as in Fig. 142.   It is quite an easy matter to work these

in at the desired intervals without upsetting the normal process of mesh-making. The bottom of these loops must be in line with the bottom of the meshes of the same row. When making the following row the shuttle is passed through this loop in just the same manner as for an ordinary mesh. The knot is tied as usual and results in an extra mesh. These loops can be added at regular distances along each row, according to the number of extra meshes required in the following row.

* * * * *

For very small meshes it is customary to use a different pattern of shuttle ; a different knot ; and, of course, a much smaller spool.

The Reef knot is used and is shown in Fig. 143. From the previous mesh the twine is brought *underneath* the spool from *behind*, passed through the loop from the *front*, round

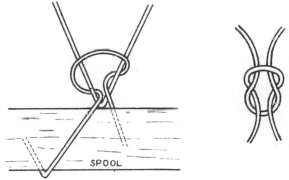

Fig. 143.   Formation of Reef Knot for Small Meshes

the front of the loop as shown, back, and through the loop again. Otherwise the process is the same as previously described.

* * * * *

There are two other ways of making a circular net. The first is very similar to that already described, except that the rows of meshes are made continuously, not finished off after each row with a reef knot. The start of the second row is rather awkward, for it is necessary to step down from the first to the second row of meshes. However, after the first few rows this fault corrects itself, and it is possible to work round in a continuous spiral without any apparent distortion of the meshes.

The other method is to make a small square of netting on the same principle as already described for a plain net. Two hooks are fixed to the wall so that this square can be hung thereon. The subsequent procedure is to work *round* the square until the net reaches the desired size. This method differs from the other in that the net is built up from the centre or bottom, rather than from the outside or top.

XI

KNOT-TYING

THERE are many purposes in angling for which different knots are required ; likewise, there are a variety of knots for each purpose. We believe that it is simpler, from the reader's point of view, to present these in groups according to the purpose for which they are intended, together with notes on the good and bad points of each, and a few directions for tying. The angler can thus select from each group the knot which most appeals to him. Opinions differ so widely that there can be no such thing as a " correct " knot ; rather, shall we say, that each knot is " suitable " for the purpose under which it is grouped.

Security is the most desirable feature in any angling knot. Unobtrusiveness and simplicity are secondary considerations, which are nevertheless important. Unfortunately, maximum security is not always possible without foregoing, to a certain extent, the other two points, but we have done our best to offer in the present selection those knots which come as nearly as possible to the ideal.

General tying instructions are as follows. Do not tie gut without first soaking until soft and pliable. Never pull a gut knot too tight. Trim off all waste ends as neatly as possible but not too close.

Knots for joining Gut or Gut-substitute

The simplest knot, but one that is far from satisfactory, is the Single Buffer or Fisherman's Knot, shown in sketch A in the illustration under the above heading. Its best points are its neatness and smallness, but these qualities are outweighed by its unreliability. However, it is used by some anglers for joining both gut and broken line.

Sketch B is a reinforced edition of A, the ends being turned twice through the loop instead of once, as in A. This gives greater security, but the best form of this knot is C—the Double Buffer. When pulled fairly tight this is slightly bulkier but is nevertheless neat and secure. It is also good for joining two lengths of line, though the neatest joint for this purpose is the splice referred to later.

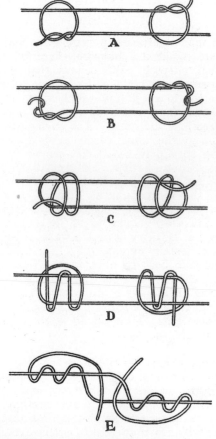

FIG. 144. KNOTS FOR JOINING GUT OR GUT SUBSTITUTE

The Barrel Knot (D) enjoys great popularity, for it is easy to tie and results in very little waste of gut. The name it bears gives a fair idea of its appearance when drawn tight. It is absolutely dependable.

But the best of all, the Blood Knot, is shown in sketch E ; it is used by professional ˙cast-makers and is no doubt chosen for its economy and complete reliability. Methods of tying vary slightly but not to any important degree. When the knot is drawn close (it must not be tight) the ends stick out from its middle. They can be snipped away with scissors, but should not be cut too close. This knot is recommended to all anglers who tie their own casts.

Knots for forming loop ends

A simple loop is shown in sketch A, but here again the knot is a little too simple to be satisfactory. It is suitable only for materials which show no great tendency to slip, such as undressed lines, etc. For a stronger knot of similar pattern the Figure-of-Eight shown in B is much better.

The disadvantages of the latter are in its bulk, and the fact that it tends to form a slight angle to the rest of the cast. It is an ideal knot however, for use on the intermediate loops of gut paternosters.

C is one of the best loops, though somewhat wasteful until the angler has had a little practice at gauging the length of gut required. After that, it is simple, neat, and " sits " well.

D and E are both good knots, the latter particularly being very economical. We are inclined to think, however, that the most satisfactory and secure is that shown in sketch C.

Knots for attaching gut loop to line.

For this purpose the knots are in every case formed in the line, around and through the gut loop.

The simplest is the Jam Hitch shown in A. In addition to the hitch made around the gut loop there is also a small knot tied in the end of the line to prevent the end from slipping through. This knot is much favoured by fly-fishermen because it is unobtrusive and quickly detachable.

Type B is much more secure but is naturally bulkier. For heavier work such as salmon or sea fishing it is preferable to the Jam Hitch.

Type C is another useful knot.   It is neat, secure, and gives good cast alignment.

D is the Helm Knot, which can be quickly detached by a sharp pull on the short end.   Apart from this detachability

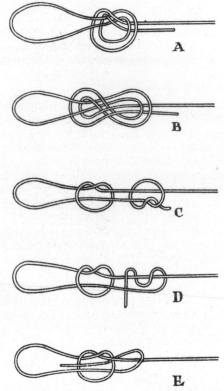

FIG. 145.   KNOTS FOR FORMING LOOP ENDS

it has nothing to recommend it ; it is neither neat nor particularly secure, but there are occasions when it can be quite useful.

When unobtrusiveness is not a major consideration the double loop attachment (E) is sometimes employed.   These loops are formed in both cast and line by using one of the loop knots previously shown. The gut loop is passed **over** the line loop and the end of the cast is drawn through the latter.

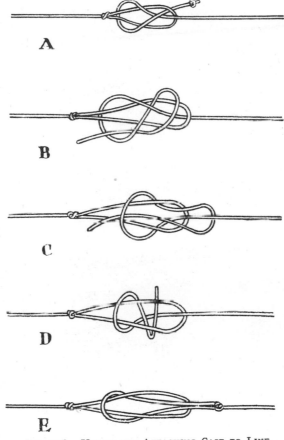

A

B

C

D

E

FIG. 146. KNOTS FOR ATTACHING CAST TO LINE

Knots for attaching gut or line to swivel.

Of the knots illustrated we prefer A and B because they embody a double turn of gut through the eye of the swivel.

This grips tightly and prevents friction which would result in wear. The latter is the better knot; its extra turn around the main length is a guarantee against slipping.

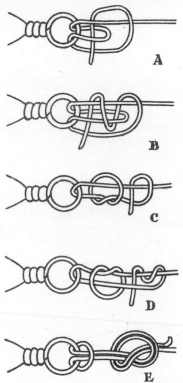

FIG. 147.   KNOTS FOR ATTACHING GUT TO SWIVEL OR EYED TREBLES

C and D are reliable knots which at first sight look very similar, but a closer inspection will reveal that the half hitch in the former is tied with the short length of gut whereas in D it is tied in the main length. Both of these should be pulled well up to the eye before drawing tight.

The loop attachment shown in E is secure but rather bulky as the gut is doubled between the swivel and the knot. The knot is tied first and the loop passed through and over the swivel afterwards. It is just as important to have the gut soft and pliable when passing over the swivel, as it is when tying the knot.

Any of the above knots can be used for attaching gut to eyed trebles.

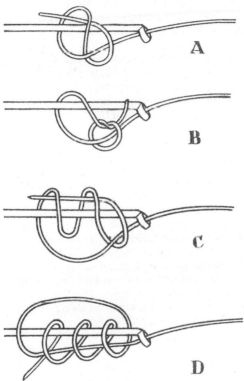

FIG. 148. KNOTS FOR ATTACHING EYED HOOK TO GUT

For methods of attaching wire to swivel the angler is referred to the chapter on " Casts and Traces."

Knots for attaching gut to eyed hooks

The inevitable Figure-of-Eight crops up again in A. The knot is reliable and neat and is therefore particularly suited to small hooks.   The waste end must not be clipped off too close.

B is a good pattern too, and has the advantage of being easy to remember. It will no doubt find favour among those who are not very adept at knot-tying.

A good strong pattern, bulkier perhaps, but absolutely dependable is shown in sketch C. It is a good intermediate between the previous knots and the pattern illustrated in D.

This latter is a real hefty knot as regards its strength and reliability but it will draw up very neatly if a little care is used when tying.   It results in very little waste of gut and, though it looks complicated, is very easy to tie. For sea anglers it is the ideal method for attaching gut to hook.

Knots for attaching gut to fly

There are more knots for this purpose than can be given in the available space. We have therefore selected five which are the most popular.

The first, A, is the single half-hitch jam knot. Nothing simpler could possibly be used, but there is some doubt about its security.   Some anglers swear by it and never use any other ; they claim that it has never failed them.   Others have used it for a time with success, then suddenly it has let them down ; always, of course, on a big fish.

It can be turned into the safer double-jam by making an extra turn through the loop (B).

A still better method is the sliding loop C. The gut is passed through the eye from the front, looped and doubled back again.   The short end is then tied in a half-hitch around the main length and is pulled just tight.   The fly is pulled downwards through the loop so that the gut lies at its head. The main length of gut is then pulled tight and everything slides snugly into position.   This knot carries the fly very nicely.

The principle of the Turle knot (D) is similar, but the half-hitch in its final position is housed behind the eye instead of in front.   Pass the gut through the eye, and form a loop by tying the short end round the main gut with a half-hitch *behind* the eye. Pull the half-hitch almost tight, pass the loop *over* the fly, and draw on the main length until the half hitch lies behind the eye and the former loop lies across its head.

The last knot, E, is named after its inventor the late Mr. A. H. E. Wood of Glassel, who also originated the

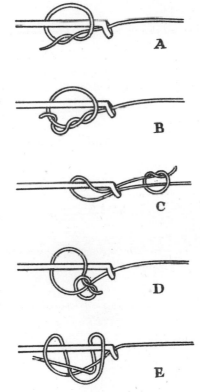

FIG. 149.   KNOTS FOR ATTACHING FLY TO GUT

"greased-line" method of salmon fishing. Though a comparatively new knot it is already widely used by salmon anglers, and particularly by those who fish by the method which Mr. Wood made famous.

Knots for attaching droppers to cast

Once again we are faced with a bewildering array from which to choose, and once again we have been guided by popularity in offering the accompanying selection.

The first is a precarious-looking but very safe attachment. It is quite practicable on all casts which are joined by sliding

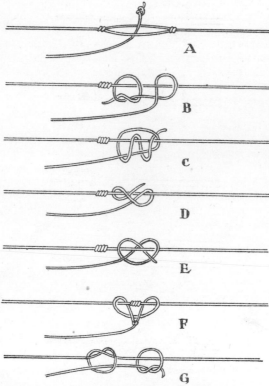

FIG. 150.   KNOTS FOR ATTACHING DROPPER TO CAST

knots such as the " fisherman's." The two halves of the knot are pulled apart and the end of the dropper-link is passed through the loop thus formed. A knot is tied in the end of the link and the whole is then drawn medium tight.

B shows another method which is very widely used. The knots in the dropper link must be made *above* a knot in the cast. This applies also to C, D and E.

Between these last mentioned there is very little to choose. All are reliable knots but must not be trimmed too closely.

In F a loop attachment is shown ; it is quite good for those who favour this style but most anglers would think it a little too cumbersome. The loop is tied first and is then wrapped round the cast above and below a knot.

G is important. It shows a safe attachment without the necessity of anchoring against a *joining* knot in the main cast. It is therefore the only method which could be used for attaching a dropper to a gut substitute cast. For anglers who use these it is especially useful.

Splicing a line

Most fly fishermen have their dressed silk casting line attached to a length of undressed backing. Some join the two ends with a knot, but this is impracticable as it is doubtful if such an obstruction will pass through the rod rings. The correct joint is a splice, which is made as follows.

Take the two ends of line which are to be joined and separate the end threads of each for about half an inch.

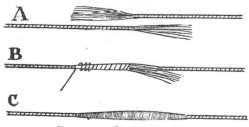

FIG. 151.   SPLICING A LINE

This fraying is easily done with a darning needle and when finished looks something like Fig. 151 A.

Lay the ends together slightly overlapping each other as seen in the same sketch and proceed to make a tight binding, starting from the middle, with well-waxed silk. The turns of this binding, though tight, should be spaced as shown in B. Having bound both ends in this manner the whole joint should be covered with a *close*, tight binding which ends in a whip finish. A smear of celluloid varnish will hold the coils in position (C).

XII

ODDS AND ENDS

THIS chapter is devoted to a few of those items of angling equipment which do not fall into any of the classes already mentioned. The odds and ends of angling are very numerous; some are useful and others are quite unnecessary. We do not propose to deal with more than a very few types.

Some of these items are so obvious and easy to make that it is quite unnecessary to give any details as to how to make them. We all know, for instance, that a serviceable fly-box can be made from a flat-fifty cigarette tin; the veriest tyro would need no instructions to guide him in dividing the tin into sections to accommodate the different patterns of fly.

The cigarette tin is again useful when making a box for spinning lures. The " 100 " size is preferable owing to its greater depth; it is divided into sections with strips of metal, wood, or cardboard.

A very effective wallet for gut casts can be made from an old bank pass-book—the type with the leather cover and the tuck-in flap. Each two pages are gummed together along their top and bottom edges with a strip of adhesive tape. It is better to do this on the " gusset " principle rather than to stick the pages tightly together, for by so doing they will open much more easily and will allow a greater space for inserting tackles.

A " priest " can easily be made by cutting a piece of metal tube to a length of eight or ten inches. The size and weight of the tube is increased in proportion to the size of the fish for which it is required.

A Line-dryer

We rather suspect that this is part of the angler's equipment which most of us manage to do without, probably because there are more vital necessities which absorb our available spare cash.   True we can dry our line by unwinding it in coils on to a sheet of newspaper laid on the floor of the spare bedroom, or we can coil it around the back of a chair, but these methods occasionally lead to disaster.

There is no satisfactory substitute for a line-dryer, but there is no need to pay 7/6 for it when one can be made at home for a few pence.

From a sheet of plywood cut four circles of six inches diameter.   An ordinary saw can be used for the purpose of cutting a rough shape, after which the corners are planed away and the edges trimmed with coarse sandpaper.

From the centre of each, using compasses, draw a circle of four inches diameter.   Using this radius (two inches) as a guide, divide the circle into six segments as shown in

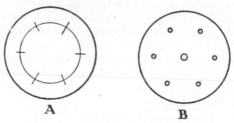

A   B

FIG. 152.   DISCS FOR LINE DRIER

Fig. 152A.   At the six points thus marked drill holes of barely $\frac{3}{8}$ inch diameter, and a hole in the centre of $\frac{1}{2}$ inch diameter.   These instructions apply to each of the four discs.

Now prepare an oblong piece of wood measuring $8\frac{1}{2}$ inches long, 4 inches wide and $\frac{3}{4}$ inch thick ; and two pieces shaped almost triangular as shown, having a base of four inches and a height of $5\frac{1}{2}$ inches.   At a point $\frac{3}{4}$ inch below the apex of each triangle drill a hole of $\frac{1}{2}$ inch diameter.

Cut six pieces of $\frac{3}{8}$ inch diameter wooden curtain rod to a length of $7\frac{7}{8}$ inches, and pass these through the holes in the discs so that a drum is formed.   These must be a tight

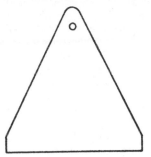

FIG. 153.   END PIECES FOR LINE DRIER

fit in the holes, and must be glued at each point where the rods pass through the discs, but the surplus glue must be scraped away lest it comes in contact with the wet line.

In the same way the centre spindle is inserted and glued, but this is eleven inches long and $\frac{1}{2}$ inch diameter.   It should project one inch from one end of the drum, and two and an eighth inches from the other end.

Pass the projecting ends through the holes in the triangular pieces of wood and screw the latter to the ends of the

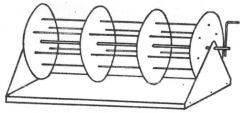

FIG. 154.   FINISHED LINE DRIER

base board.   If so desired an improvement can be made by inserting a couple of thick metal washers between the end discs and the triangular uprights.

It will be seen that one end of the centre spindle now

projects about one inch from the triangular upright. Bore a hole of $\frac{3}{16}$ inch diameter crosswise through this end, and glue into it a piece of metal rod of as tight a fit as possible, bent previously at right angles as shown. This forms the handle and completes the line-dryer.

The type thus made will accommodate three lines at once. If more or less are required the reader can make the necessary adjustments in design.

For best results it is advisable to screw the baseboard to a bench or other fixed surface.

A Gaff and holder

Anyone can make a gaff but most anglers make them too heavy. At least, the river type as used for salmon and pike are usually rather cumbersome. The gaff we are about to describe is light but strong, small but effective, and is combined with a gaff-holder which is the most efficient which we have yet seen. This holder, of course, is necessary only when the angler is continually on the move as in river fishing. In a boat it is absolutely unnecessary, but in any case a heavier gaff would be required for boat fishing.

For the gaff itself, the materials are a 30 inch length of $\frac{1}{2}$ inch ash, greenheart or hickory, (the thicker end of an old golf club shaft is ideal if not required for very heavy fish) ; a 10/0 or 12/0 O'Shaughnessy hook, a length of plated copper wire for whipping, a length of thin cord, and a small brass screw.

Slightly flatten the last two inches of the hook-end of

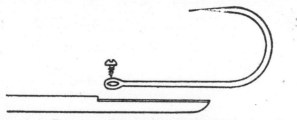

FIG. 155. SECURING HOOK TO GAFF

your handle with a rasp or chisel. This provides a snug seating for the hook. Now round off the extreme end so that it cannot get stuck when withdrawing from the holder. So far the business end of the gaff looks like Fig. 155 which also shows the hook and screw ready to be fixed in position.

Before fitting however, the barb of the hook should be filed away, after which it can be secured in the position shown. It is here that the necessity for the O'Shaughnessy type of hook becomes apparent, for the eye is in the same

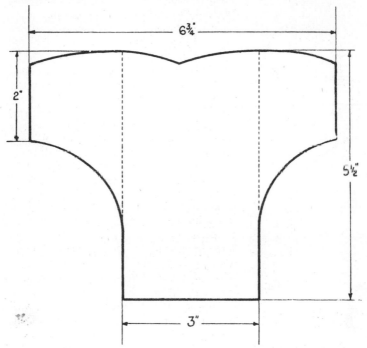

FIG. 156. CUT-OUT SHAPE FOR GAFF CARRIER

plane as the shank and will lie perfectly on the prepared flat surface of the handle.

After screwing down the hook take the copper wire and commence to bind the hook to the shank by a whipping. This should start from the extreme end and should finish when it reaches the eye.

The part where the hand grips should then be bound with thin cord to prevent slipping when the handle is wet. A coat of varnish and the gaff is complete.

Now for the holder. Take a piece of fairly stout leather and cut it into the shape shown in Fig. 156. Fold it over and stitch along the dotted lines shown in the following sketch. Cut a small button-holed tab from another piece of leather and stitch this on in the position indicated.

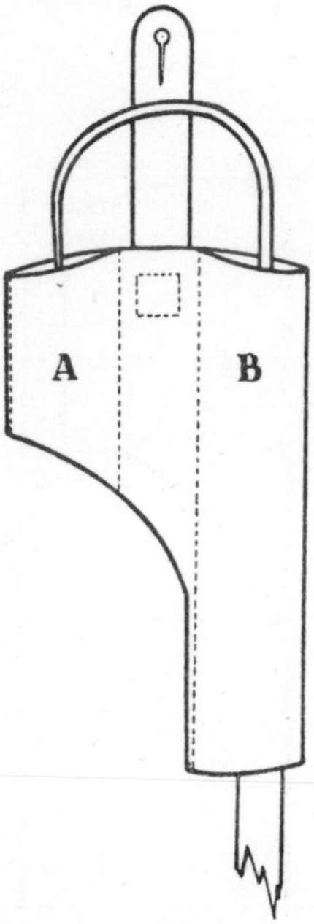

Into division A insert a cork which fits tightly. This is intended to receive the point of the gaff. Shape division B so that it is rounded and tubular in form, and will thus readily admit the gaff handle. This completes the job.

Imagine the holder buttoned to the coat at a little over waist height. Push the handle end of the gaff into slide B to its fullest extent until the point rests on the cork in A. A slight extra push will drive the hook point securely into the cork where the gaff is firmly held until required (Fig. 157).

Both hands are thus left absolutely free until a fish is played out. Then, simply ease the hook point from the cork and lift straight upwards. If you have left a generous clearance in division B this will be the simplest and quickest process imaginable.

FIG. 157. GAFF IN
FINISHED CARRIER

Stronger gaffs, for heavy work at sea, are best made from the type of hook illustrated in Fig. 158. At the end of the shank is a spike which projects at a right-angle. When embedded into the handle and whipped, there is no danger of the hook turning or coming adrift. A further improvement can be made by cutting a groove in the wood for the shank to lie in, though this is not absolutely essential.

All sea gaffs should embody a loop made of cord or thong leather, which is passed through a hole bored in the end of the handle. This will give a very secure grip and, if properly used, will make it almost impossible for the gaff to be wrenched from the hand.

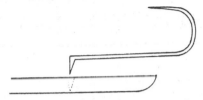

FIG. 158. ATTACHMENT FOR HEAVY GAFF

The method is the same as that used by the police in gripping their truncheons and is illustrated in Fig. 159. The thumb is first passed through the loop, which is then wrapped round the back of the hand to the palm, in which

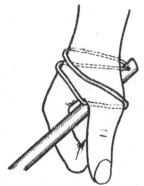

FIG. 159. HOW TO USE LEATHER THONG LOOP

the handle is gripped. The loop should be of just sufficient length to fit closely round the hand between the gaff handle and the thumb. Thus a downward pull from a heavy fish, which might normally pull the handle out of one's grip, is checked by the loop anchored round the thumb.

Rod Rests

Most of the rod rests illustrated can be made from mild steel rod of $\frac{1}{4}$ inch diameter, which can easily be bent to any desired shape.

To make type A a length of the rod is bent into a letter
U, the parallel sides of which are each about twelve inches

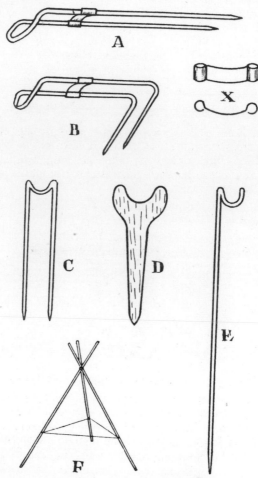

FIG. 160. TYPES OF ROD RESTS

long and 1¾ inches apart.   Place the bottom of the U in the
vice and bend the remainder over until it assumes the shape

A. Now cut a strip of zinc or tin and bend it into shape X so that it will slide along the parallel " legs " of the rod rest. File each end to a point so that they can be driven into the ground. The angle at which the rod is held over the water can be increased or decreased by sliding X along the legs.

Type B is made in exactly the same way but requires a slightly longer piece of metal to allow for the extra bend. This is a very satisfactory pattern but does not pack away so nicely as type A. Both these rod-rests have one very useful feature—they are not only " rod-rests " but they are also " rod-grips " ; they will hold a rod in position without the necessity (as in the following patterns) of the butt end resting on the river bank. Thus almost the whole length of the rod can be held over the water whereas on the other types at least two feet must be lying on the bank. Fig. 161 will make this clear.

Type C is so simple that no explanation is necessary. The metal is of the same thickness and the " legs " are about a foot long.

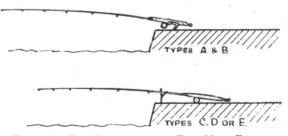

FIG. 161. THE EFFECT OF THE TWO MAIN TYPES

D is the same sort of thing made from wood and is, if anything, preferable to the previous pattern. A tough wood, such as ash, should be used and should be finished smoothly in the cup where the rod is to lie.

Types E and F are favoured more by sea-anglers for beach fishing. The former is our familiar mild steel bar with the top bent into a hook to accommodate the rod. The lower end is sharpened to a point to assist penetration into the sand. The usual height is three feet.

Three ordinary garden canes and a length of stout string are all the materials for making F. The canes may be anything from two feet to four feet in length. At a point six inches from their upper end bind them together to form a tripod ; then secure the string between the three legs at equal distances apart—this will prevent slipping. Thus you have a rod rest which will answer perfectly on all sorts of beach surfaces, and will collapse at a touch when it is time to pack up.

INDEX